THE EVERYTHING

DOG BREED GUIDES

A S THE OWNER of a particular type of dog—or someone who is thinking about adopting one—you probably have some questions about that dog breed that can't be answered anywhere else. In particular, you want to know what breed-specific health issues and behavioral traits might arise as you plan for the future with your beloved canine family member.

THE EVERYTHING® DOG BREED GUIDES give you clear-cut answers to all your pressing questions. These authoritative books give you all you need to know about identifying common characteristics; choosing the right puppy or adult dog; coping with personality quirks; instilling obedience; and raising your pet in a healthy, positive environment.

THE EVERYTHING® DOG BREED GUIDES are an extension of the bestselling EVERYTHING® series in the pets category, which include *The Everything® Dog Book* and *The Everything® Dog Training and Tricks Book*. These authoritative, family-friendly books are specially designed to be one-stop guides for anyone looking to explore a specific breed in depth.

Visit the entire *Everything*® series at www.everything.com

THE EVERYTHING

German Shepherd Book

Dear Reader:

The decision to bring a new dog into your life is a big one. When the addition is a German shepherd, the decision is even bigger! This breed comes with a lot of responsibility. But when the right shepherd is matched with the right home, the advantages are endless. In this book, I've included everything you need to know to determine if this incredible breed is for you, and, if so, how to give your new shepherd the care and environment she needs to thrive.

For those of you who already own a shepherd, or who have owned shepherds all your lives, I've tried to include interesting tidbits of information from a variety of sources. It is my hope that somewhere in these pages, you'll recognize aspects of the German shepherd that you already know (and love), as well as find and come away with lots of new and exciting information.

I hope this book is helpful to you and that you enjoy reading it. If you implement the knowledge and experience imparted here, you and your shepherd are sure to have a long and happy life together. Enjoy!

With best regards,

Joan H. Wal

THE
EVERYTHING®
GERMAN SHEPHERD BOOK

A complete guide to raising, training,
and caring for your German shepherd

Joan Hustace Walker

Adams Media
Avon, Massachusetts

Dedication:
This book is dedicated to EPD K-9, "Rocky," and to all those noble
shepherds that have come before him and will follow in the future.

Publishing Director: Gary M. Krebs
Managing Editor: Kate McBride
Copy Chief: Laura M. Daly
Acquisitions Editor: Kate Burgo
Development Editor: Katie McDonough
Production Editors: Jamie Wielgus,
Bridget Brace

Director of Manufacturing: Susan Beale
Associate Director of Production: Michelle Roy Kelly
Series Designers: Daria Perreault and John Paulhus
Cover Design: Paul Beatrice, Erick DaCosta,
Matt LeBlanc
Layout and Graphics: Colleen Cunningham,
Holly Curtis, Erin Dawson, Sorae Lee

An Everything® Series Book.
Everything® and everything.com® are registered trademarks of F+W Publications, Inc.

Published by Adams Media, an F+W Publications Company
57 Littlefield Street, Avon, MA 02322 U.S.A.
www.adamsmedia.com

ISBN: 1-59337-424-0

Printed in Canada.
J I H G F E D C B A

Library of Congress Cataloging-in-Publication Data
Walker, Joan Hustace
The everything German shepherd book : a complete guide to raising, training, and caring for
your German shepherd / Joan Hustace Walker.
p. cm. -- (An everything series book)
Includes bibliographical references and index.
ISBN 1-59337-424-0
1. German shepherd dog. I. Title. II. Series: Everything series.
SF429.G37W34 2005
636.737'6--dc22

2005017398

Cover photo ©Kaelson, Carol J. / Animals Animals / Earth Scenes
Interior Photographs: Jean Fogle Photography

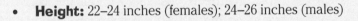

BREED SPECIFICATIONS

- **Height:** 22–24 inches (females); 24–26 inches (males)

- **Weight:** 65 to 95 pounds

- **Head:** Long, wedge-shaped muzzle; sloping head; moderately arched forehead

- **Ears:** Moderately pointed, open toward the front

- **Feet:** Short, compact, well-arched toes

- **Tail:** Bushy, hangs in a slight curve

- **Coat:** Medium-length double coat

- **Topline:** Shoulders slope into a straight, strong back

- **Movement:** Effortless, long, and smooth trot

- **Temperament:** Self-confident, alert, and intelligent; can be exceptionally gentle with small children if raised with them; protective and territorial, with a tendency to "overdo" these traits if not well socialized with people and dogs

Acknowledgments

This book would not have been possible without the generous help and experience of so many German shepherd experts. My thanks go out to Christiane and Konrad Ostermeier, Tish Walker, Cliff Weaver, Mary Davis, Andrea Portbury, Jim Matarese, Jim Elder, Ed Johnson, Judy Grumdahl, and Christine Neering, D.V.M. Also, very special thanks to Tim Nussmeier for his kind help with this and all my German shepherd projects. Thanks, also, to Randy, Eric, Grace, Lani, Curtis, and my parents, who haven't missed a book signing yet.

. . .

Contents

Chapter 16: Teaching the Basics 201

Chapter 17: Basic Dog Health Care 215

Chapter 18: Advanced Care................... 229

Introduction

THE GERMAN SHEPHERD IS A WIDELY LOVED and cherished breed. This dog has many wonderful traits that draw you in, but if you don't know much about shepherds, you may be in for a surprise. When a person purchases a shepherd without knowing the ins and outs of the breed, the experience is often an unpleasant one. Most shepherds are not "bad" dogs; they can be perfectly delightful companions. However, unless you know what makes a shepherd a shepherd, you may mistake certain behaviors for flaws or problems.

The German shepherd is definitely not the dog for everyone. This breed requires a lot of time and effort, particularly during the dog's first three years of life. Daily training, handling, and extensive socialization with all kinds of people and dogs are not optional; these are mandatory if you are to succeed with this breed.

However, shepherds do make outstanding companions, competitors, and family pets when raised by those who understand the breed. The owner who recognizes this dog's need for exercise, training, and mental stimulation is well equipped to care for a shepherd. This owner will experience all the intelligence, loyalty, and undying devotion this breed has to offer.

German shepherds that aren't given an outlet for their energy, however, can become destructive. The owner of a shepherd must always be attentive to prevent the development of this trait. This dog also needs an owner who is willing to work on socializing her with all kinds of people and dogs and continue this training throughout the dog's life. This is a breed that can regress or become less outgoing and trusting if she is not constantly out and about, in the company of others.

This breed also requires quite a bit of training. Training not only keeps a shepherd mentally stimulated and makes a large, strong dog manageable, it also helps serve as a gentle daily reminder as to who is the leader in the dog-human relationship.

When selecting a shepherd, your primary concern is to choose a dog with an outstanding temperament. It's hard to mold a puppy into the adult dog you want unless you begin with a puppy with the potential to be a well-tempered dog. Due to the German shepherd's rapid rise in popularity decades ago, as well as his current position as one of the most popular breeds in the country, these dogs have suffered at the hands of breeders who are only out to capitalize on this popularity. Every year, many German shepherd puppies are bred only for looks and, thus, end up with some strange temperaments.

Poorly bred shepherds also tend to suffer from all kinds of health problems. So even if you do find a German shepherd with a nice temperament, the dog might still come to suffer from illnesses that require expensive treatment. Veterinary medicine is wonderful, but it can only do so much.

These drawbacks may seem daunting, but they are easily overcome. This book will help you learn about this beloved breed, guide you in your research, and show you what to look for in a breeder and a shepherd. With some information, time, and patience, you'll be ready to enjoy years of fun with your new friend.

An International Hero

THE GERMAN SHEPHERD IS RECOGNIZED world-wide for his remarkable courage, loyalty, and ability to work in virtually any situation with intelligence and an unparalleled eagerness to please. However, this breed is more than an outstanding working dog; he is also a treasured family pet and companion.

Historic Herder

The German shepherd is descended from the best herding dogs found in Germany. As a result, the progenitors of today's German shepherd were found in a variety of colors: white, sable, tan and black, solid black, and brindle. The coat type also varied from short- to longhaired, and there were even wirehaired dogs. Some dogs' ears stood erect; other dogs' ears may have flopped over. Some shepherd dogs held their tails low; others had tails curling over their backs.

Centuries ago, it didn't matter what the shepherd looked like, as long as he had the instincts and drive to perform his herding job. Of course, the German shepherd varied from other herding breeds. He was not only asked to "tend" the sheep but also protect them from wolves, bears, and enterprising humans.

The shepherd's job as a "tender" involved keeping large flocks of sheep (sometimes more than 100 animals) contained on the owner's grazing land. Tending differs from other forms of herding. The dog essentially circles the flock to keep it contained and moves the flock forward as the sheepherder might direct. With few, if any, fences erected in Germany before the end of the nineteenth century, herding dogs with tending capabilities were critically important.

Fact

Though the ancestors of the German shepherd are often referred to as "German shepherds," the purebred form of this dog you recognize today did not evolve until the late 1800s.

In the barnyard, the German shepherds were called upon to help with small groups of sheep, separating and holding them as needed for medical attention, sheering, and other procedures. Once these chores were completed, the shepherd was often directed to gather the sheep and move them down narrow roads or through towns toward the market. The early canine shepherds of Germany truly were a versatile breed, performing chores that several specialized herding breeds (and livestock guardian breeds) were used for in other countries.

But the shepherd's position as sheep tender would not last forever. As the world changed, so did this breed. Near the end of the nineteenth century, when fences were erected and rail travel became an efficient way to transport livestock, herding dogs were no longer needed in great numbers. Though some breeds of herding dogs vanished, Germans recognized that, in addition to its extraordinary herding abilities, the German shepherd had great potential to do other kinds of work.

At this time, there were three different types of shepherds that appeared in Germany, each associated with a different region.

Shepherds from Wurttemberg appeared in a variety of colors and had beautiful tails that were carried lower, as opposed to curling over the dogs' backs. Shepherds from the Thuringia region did not appear in the variety of colors that the Wurttemberg dogs did; rather, they were predominantly wolf gray. The Thuringia shepherds were distinctive because they had consistently erect, well-placed ears. The third group of shepherds, from Swabia, was mostly noted for its herding characteristics, which translated into ability to navigate difficult terrain. This shepherd had great agility, endurance, strength, and speed.

 **Essential**

Herding breeds were sometimes considered for positions as police and military dogs during the late 1800s and early 1900s. In Germany, one of the favored breeds for this work was the smooth collie.

Max von Stephanitz—now often referred to as the father of the German shepherd breed—worked with other breeders to develop a purebred dog with the best qualities from the three German shepherd varieties. In just ten years, from 1889 to 1899, von Stephanitz and Germany's shepherd breeders were able to create a true purebred—one that appeared primarily within the set breed standards without any extreme variations.

In 1899, von Stephanitz founded the Verein Für Deutsche Schäferhunde (SV), Germany's German shepherd club. That same year, the SV approved a breed standard, and the world's oldest German shepherd registry was opened.

War Dog

Von Stephanitz, a captain in the German army's cavalry, felt that the versatile German shepherd had great potential as a police dog as well as a war dog. He was right. The German shepherd's history as both a military and police dog is exemplary. The breed's skills and accomplishments have set the standard for all other working breeds for more than a century.

Prussian Service

Impressed by work performed by police dogs in England (Airedales), the Imperial Prussian Army subsidized the formation of training clubs to develop top-notch war dogs. A wide range of dog breeds were being used at the time, including gun dogs, poodles, Airedales, farm collies (called smooth collies today), Dobermans, and German shepherds. The dogs were trained as sentries, messengers, and medic dogs, also known as Red Cross dogs, comfort dogs, or Sanitätshunde.

 **Fact**

Medic dogs were trained to pull off the Bringsel, a sort of short leash that was part of the Prussian uniform, from a wounded soldier and bring it to a medic. The dog then led the medic to the soldier. While the soldier was being treated, the medic dog would comfort the injured—hence, the name "comfort dogs."

German shepherds were so good at the varied work they were required to perform that in 1887, General von Goltz supposedly recommended discontinuing the use of all other breeds. However, his recommendation was not enacted.

World War I

The German army began World War I with 6,000 trained military dogs, many of which were German shepherds. Germany also called on loyal German shepherd owners and breeders to offer trained dogs for the war cause. By the end of the war, it is estimated that more than 30,000 dogs served in Germany's army.

German shepherds were used during the war in many capacities. The dogs delivered messages to maintain communications and carried ammunition and medical supplies in backpacks. Shepherds also guarded and herded livestock that was kept near the front lines to feed Germany's army. Perhaps the German shepherd's most famous position was as a sentry (stationary alert) and a scout (moving alert) dog. The dogs didn't bark but rather quietly whined or growled to alert their handlers that someone was approaching. German shepherds also patrolled prison camps to prevent prisoners from escaping or communicating with their comrades.

Both the French and British armies also trained and used German shepherds for military service, though in much smaller numbers than the German army. The dogs used by the Allies performed similarly to their German counterparts, and they did so with unswerving loyalty and courage.

 **Question?**

Why was a British shepherd named Tommy awarded the Croix de Guerre by the French army?
While serving valiantly as a military K-9 in World War I, Tommy was wounded three times. He also narrowly survived being gassed after his handler, who was working for his Scottish regiment, didn't get Tommy's mask on quickly enough.

It would be years before the German shepherd flourished again in Germany as it had during the Great War. Thousands of German shepherds, as well as many noted breeders, were killed during the conflict. Additionally, near the end of the war, the country suffered a tremendous famine, causing both people and dogs to starve.

For the German shepherds that survived the war and the famine in Germany, there were more hurdles to overcome. Surviving shepherds were often sterile or gave birth to higher numbers of stillborns.

Postwar veterinary care and access to medicine was virtually non-existent. As a result, canine diseases ran rampant. Still, German shepherd breeders in Germany—and in the United States, England, and many European countries—worked to restore the breed.

World War II

The entire world witnessed the abilities of the German shepherd during World War I. Americans serving in the armed forces told incredible tales of the dogs they had seen; some even brought puppies and adult dogs home with them. As a result, the breed began rising in popularity as a canine companion in the United States. Despite having seen the magnificent work of the German shepherds, however, the United States military did not institute a war-dog program after World War I, and they entered World War II without experienced dog handlers, trainers, or an active training facility.

 Essential

American Corporal Lee Duncan and other members of the 136th Aero Division were on a scouting mission when Duncan discovered five German shepherd puppies at an abandoned German war-dog station. Duncan's pup, Rinty, became the unit's mascot and, later, one of the country's most beloved canine movie stars: Rin Tin Tin.

At the first rumblings of war in Germany, breeders were immediately concerned with the future of their prized shepherds. Some breeders discretely shipped their esteemed dogs out of the country. Breeders from urban areas—remembering the food shortage of the past war—tried to move their dogs to area farms where it was hoped that food would remain more plentiful. Others reportedly euthanized their dogs as an alternative to slow starvation.

Nevertheless, Nazi Germany began rebuilding its trained war-dog program under the guise of police-dog training. When World War II began, Germany was estimated to have more than 200,000 dogs trained and ready for military work, the majority of which were German shepherds.

Back in the United States, even after entering the war, military leaders weren't convinced the military dog could be of any benefit in a war without trenches. In fact, it took an aggressive civilian group, Dogs for Defense, to prod the military into working with quality dogs (donated by owners and breeders) and train under experienced, volunteer dog trainers.

Within months, dogs were guarding civilian war plants and quartermaster depots. The experimental program soon expanded to include trained sentry, patrol, messenger, and mine-detection dogs.

Alert!

The Marine Devil Dogs of World War II are often remembered as Doberman pinschers; however, three German shepherds were members of the First Marine Dog Platoon. In fact, a large male German shepherd in this platoon, Caesar, carried the first war-dog message in a conflict in the Pacific.

The United States initially used more than thirty breeds for military work, but by the fall of 1942, the list was pared down to seven breeds, with the German shepherd a number-one choice. One service branch, the coast guard, used only female German shepherds on their beach patrols.

The tasks that the German shepherd was asked to perform during World War II were very similar to those assigned in World War I. There were a few unusual positions, such as the British "para pups"—military dogs that were trained to parachute with England's airborne army and SAS units. The dogs also helped the soldiers detect the enemy while working behind enemy lines.

One shepherd, Brian, was attached to a British parachute battalion that landed in Normandy. Later, Great Britain awarded Brian the Dickin Medal for gallantry and devotion to duty. Brian also became a fully qualified paratrooper based on his number of successful jumps.

🐕 Fact

The German shepherd's name has changed many times throughout the centuries around the world. For example, during World War II, the German shepherd was referred to as the Alsatian Wolf Dog in England and as the Shepherd Dog in the United States.

Though the German shepherd served valiantly on both sides during World War II, the massive loss of canine life in Germany was devastating. Fortunately, those who loved these dogs showed the same courage, ingenuity, and tenacity as their beloved breed. German breeders, as well as those in Great Britain, other parts of Europe, and the United States, once again helped the German shepherd rise above adversity.

Post-World War II

After hostilities ceased, the American military downsized its military dog program and found itself with thousands of war dogs without jobs. The dogs were shipped back to the United States and returned to their original owners. If the owners were deceased, the reactivated Dogs for Defense assisted in placing the dogs in homes. Dogs for Defense received more than 17,000 requests to adopt roughly 3,000 homeless war dogs. Of all those placed in homes, only four were reportedly returned due to inappropriate behavior.

In 1951, when aggression broke out in Korea, U.S. scout-dog platoons were called into action. The dogs, primarily German shepherds, were extremely successful. One shepherd, York, was given a distinguished service award for performing 148 combat patrols.

From 1960 to 1975, German shepherds served in the U.S. military, primarily as patrol and sentry dogs. In 1965, the first military dogs and handlers were sent to Vietnam. Five years later, when American troops were returning home, military dog handlers were told that their dogs—who had served so valiantly beside them—could not return. It is estimated that the number of dogs left in Vietnam numbered more than 1,000, with fewer than 120 dogs making it back to the states. (The U.S. Marine Corps did find ways to bring back all their dogs.)

 **Essential**

The forced abandonment of dogs in Vietnam so affected dog handlers that they banded together to prevent this from happening again. Today, no dog is left behind, and rather than euthanizing dogs once they are too old to serve, the military is working to place these valuable dogs with experienced dog handlers and their families.

Today's military dog is multifaceted. Some German shepherds are trained as patrol dogs, whereas others work primarily as narcotics and/or explosives detection dogs. Due to the breed's versatility and ability to understand the commands and body language of several different handlers, the German shepherd will likely remain one of the military's chief resources.

Police K-9 and Service Dog

The German shepherd has reigned as the top choice in the United States for K-9 police work for more than a half a century. As a police dog, the German shepherd is often trained for patrol work, which can include such skills as tracking suspects, finding lost people, checking buildings for occupants, and chasing down and holding a criminal or suspect.

Though the public's perception of a police K-9 is often one of a German shepherd gnashing his teeth against a side window of a police patrol car, the typical K-9 is usually very friendly with people. Police dogs go home each day with their handlers, easily making the transition from working dog to family dog.

As police K-9s, German shepherds are often trained to detect narcotics and/or explosives. In the role of detection dog, the German shepherd is trained for either passive alerts (a sit or down, with the dog indicating the find by pointing at the area with its head and gaze) or an aggressive alert (scratching and barking at the location of the find). Explosives detection dogs use a passive alert, for obvious reasons, and narcotics detection dogs may use either a passive or an aggressive alert.

 **Fact**

In addition to the police, German shepherds serve many government agencies, such as the U.S. Border Patrol, U.S. State Department, U.S. Department of Agriculture, the Federal Bureau of Investigation, Central Intelligence Agency, Bureau of Alcohol, Tobacco, and Firearms, National Transportation Safety Board, federal penitentiaries, and the Washington Park Police.

German shepherds have also been (and continue to be) incredible service dogs. During World War I, many soldiers lost their vision through injuries from shrapnel, grenades, or gunfire, as well as exposure to poisonous gases. After the war, Germany trained its shepherds to serve as guide dogs for injured veterans— an idea that was quickly taken up by the United States.

Today, German shepherds are employed in many different areas of service. They are used as hearing dogs for the deaf (alerting their handlers to specific sounds), mobility assistance dogs (helping the handler negotiate obstacles while in a wheelchair), seizure alert dogs (detecting oncoming seizures), service dogs (assisting the handler in performing everyday tasks, such as picking up dropped pencils, credit cards, etc.), and therapy dogs (assisting patients to improve or maintain cognitive or physical functioning in a wide range of hospital, long-term care, physical therapy, psychiatric, and educational settings).

Additionally, the German shepherd is perhaps one of the most talented search and rescue (SAR) breeds to serve the community. Trained for wilderness and urban life rescues, as well as cadaver searches, the German shepherd has proven to be a focused and tireless worker for civilian volunteer SAR handlers, as well as firefighter, police, and other first-responder SAR handlers.

 **Essential**

After the terrorist attacks of September 11, 2001, the German shepherd once again proved to be one of this country's most valuable assets. Both civilian and public service agencies used German shepherds to search for survivors and remains, providing many families with desperately needed closure.

Without a doubt, the German shepherd will continue to be a top choice for service work and will most likely be a preferred candidate for emerging fields, such as psychiatric assistance, in the future.

Breed Clubs

Many different clubs have been formed over the past years to support one or more aspects of the German shepherd. Some clubs are geared toward sport dogs (Schutzhund, or as renamed in 2004, Vielseitigkeitspruefung für Gebrauchshunde [VPG], which means "working dog sport"). These clubs are focused on training for competitions that include tracking, obedience, and protection. Using play drives and positive reinforcement, they are trained to grab and hold the padded arm of the helper, or training assistant. For these dogs, the protection phase of Schutzhund competition is a game. If a person's arm is not padded and the dog is ordered to attack that individual, the German shepherd is likely to do nothing except become very confused.

Other associations, such as the United States Police Canine Association and the Canadian Police Canine Association, are specifically for working K-9s. Working shepherds, those serving in the military, police, and other government agencies, require all the drives and characteristics that the sport shepherd possesses, and then some. Specifically, K-9s must possess a higher level of confidence than sport dogs to execute their training in totally unfamiliar scenarios, not just practice fields in which the testing setup is always the same. K-9s must be trustworthy and friendly in large crowds of people, but they must also be able to switch into protection mode at a signal from the handler or if the handler is attacked.

Verein Für Deutsche Schäferhunde (SV)

In addition to serving as the oldest German shepherd registry in the world (started in 1899), the SV offers conformation shows, Schutzhund trials, and "breed surveys," in which a dog is tested to see if she has the correct temperament and drive to work as a K-9.

German Shepherd Club of America

The German Shepherd Dog Club of America (GSDCA) is the U.S. parent club for the German shepherd. It is not a registry—dogs are registered through the American Kennel Club. As the parent breed club, it is the club that is recognized by the AKC. The GSDCA was formed in 1913 and was incorporated in 1916.

Working Dog Association

The Working Dog Association (WDA), founded in 1982, is an offshoot of the GSDCA. The purpose of the WDA is to promote the "total" dog: the German shepherd that can do it all—succeed in working trials as well as in the conformation ring. The WDA hosts Schutzhund trials, conformation shows, and breed surveys.

DVG-America

The Deutscher Verband der Gebrauchshundsportvereine (DVG), or The German Club for the Working Sport Dog, was founded in Germany in 1947. The DVG is dedicated to the sport of Schutzhund and is not a registry. The branch of the DVG in the United States is called the DVG-America.

United Schutzhund Clubs of America

The United Schutzhund Clubs of America (USA) emphasizes the total, working German shepherd. It holds Schutzhund trials, conformation shows, and breed surveys. Both the GSDCA's and the USA's breed standards closely follow that of the SV.

The Pain of Popularity

The German shepherd continues to be one of the most popular purebreds in the United States. Because of movies featuring German shepherds in heroic roles, such as Strongheart and Rin Tin Tin, the breed has received enormous media attention. While this attention may seem positive, the breed's wide exposure has resulted in a significant problem.

 Fact

The German shepherd hit the #1 breed registration ranking with the AKC in the late 1920s and has remained in the top ten since that time. The shepherd is also one of the most common breeds to be seen in shelters and pounds.

When people saw an intelligent, handsome, perfectly obedient dog on the big screen, they immediately wanted to own a German shepherd. However, the supply of well-bred, quality German shepherds was minimal compared to the soaring demand. So people who had no knowledge of the breed cashed in on the latest fad and began breeding German shepherds as fast as the public could scoop them up.

As a result, the 1960s and 1970s were flooded with poorly bred shepherds, who were inherently at higher risk for genetic diseases and temperament disorders. Additionally, since so many people had a romanticized and unrealistic image of the breed, this energetic working dog wound up in homes unsuited for its true nature.

Before long, the criminal portion of society realized that the German shepherd's intelligence and trainability could be used for unlawful purposes. This exploitation caused a swing in public opinion about the dogs that lingers even today. When the breed's courage and loyalty were used for the wrong reasons, the German shepherd became the first "bad" dog in the country; these dogs were responsible for a disproportionate number of bites and fatalities in the 1970s. The general public came to fear and abandon the breed.

While a number of other breeds have since taken over the spot of criminal accomplice, the thoughtless breeding of shepherds does continue, as do sales to the wrong owners.

The German Shepherd Today

After suffering so long at the hands of the inept and the illicit, where does the German shepherd stand today as a potential canine companion? Currently, potential German shepherd owners will find an array of temperaments (from the very good to the very bad), different levels of energy (from highly active to relaxed companions), a variety of conformation (from near perfection to something that might be confused with a shepherd mix), and a mixed bag as far as health.

But before you panic that the search for a German shepherd will be too taxing, take heart in knowing there *are* excellent breeders and quality puppies and dogs out there. The goal is to find a conscientious breeder who values dogs with balanced temperaments and outstanding health—with conformation and soundness ranking a very close second.

▲ Your typical German shepherd

Is This the Dog for You?

All who know and love the German shepherd will readily admit that the breed is not for everyone. And, though veteran German shepherd owners regularly take the breed's challenges in stride, those who are new to the breed may be surprised or alarmed by some of the shepherd's characteristics. If you are considering owning a German shepherd, it's best to become familiar with both the pros and the cons associated with this dog.

Things You'll Love

The German shepherd can be a fantastic companion to all kinds of people. The following are some of the positive traits this breed carries:

- Loyal
- Courageous
- Protective of family
- Gentle with children
- Gets along well with other pets
- Plays nicely with other dogs

- Intelligent
- Easy to train
- Long-lived (12 to 14 years)
- Athletic
- Versatile; can compete in many performance events
- Easily washable coat
- Adaptable to small and large homes
- Expressive
- Playful

Unpleasant Aspects

While German shepherds make great pets when well-bred and given the proper care, some dogs still exhibit challenging traits and habits, including:

- Tendency to escape
- Compulsive chewing
- Destructiveness when bored or lacking exercise
- Not suited to living only outdoors
- High activity level
- Demanding of attention
- Requires training throughout life
- Frequent barker; uses lots of vocal communication
- Significant shedding, especially during change of seasons
- Severe separation anxiety*
- Overly protective*
- Overly territorial*
- Aggressive toward other dogs*
- Aggressive toward people*
- Unpredictable biting**
- Nervous, anxious**
- Fearful, fear biting**
- Poor hips; high rate of hip dysplasia**
- High rate of spondylosis**
- Allergies/skin problems**

*Many of these traits can be moderated or prevented entirely with good socialization skills and training from an early age.

**These traits are most often found in poorly bred German shepherds and can be avoided almost entirely by purchasing a puppy from a quality breeder or adopting an adult German shepherd from a reputable breed rescue.

Weighing the Good and the Bad

No breed is perfect. Furthermore, no individual dog is perfect. Every breed and every dog have characteristics that can challenge any owner. The questions you need to ask yourself are these: How challenging will owning a German shepherd be for *you*? How challenging will this dog be for your family? For your significant other? Can you meet this breed's specific needs? Are you willing to change those things in your life or lifestyle that *don't* match a German shepherd's needs?

 **Essential**

The correct name of the breed in the United States is German Shepherd Dog (GSD). The German shepherd is the only breed to have the word "dog" as part of its full name. When reading about this breed you will commonly see the acronym GSD used to refer to this breed.

If you find the German shepherd *is* the right dog for you, and you are ready and willing to invest the time, money, and patience involved, your efforts will be rewarded tenfold with the experience of a great pet. When good dogs are paired with good people, there really is no other breed like the German shepherd.

Depending on your rescued adult's temperament, you may consider training and certifying him for animal-assisted therapy work. A good German shepherd that has the capacity to enter almost any situation without trepidation and really enjoys being around people would be a perfect choice for this work.

Question?

Is it true that service dogs and police K-9s often come from shelters?
At one time, most service dogs and police K-9s were rescued from shelters and pounds. Today, some trainers still find great working-dog candidates in abandoned pets, but many turn to breeders instead.

Rescued dogs have also done well as search-and-rescue (SAR) dogs. German shepherds have the natural ability to track and trail scents. Those dogs that are particularly toy motivated—they can't get enough of playing with a ball or tugging on a rolled-up towel—tend to respond to this training exceptionally well. An SAR dog must be passive around unfamiliar dogs and people, since much of SAR work is performed off lead.

Sources for Adult Dogs

Shelters, pounds, and breed rescues are usually inundated with German shepherds that need placement. However, there are some additional sources for adult dogs that you might consider.

From time to time, a respected, reputable breeder may have a young adult dog for sale. It could be that the breeder has held back this dog as a show prospect, but the dog didn't quite develop the way he'd hoped. Sometimes a dog will suffer an injury that swiftly ends her show or competitive career. Or perhaps the breeder was training a puppy in Schutzhund or K-9 work, but during more advanced training, it became obvious that the dog lacked the necessary drives for these specialized jobs.

If a breeder has kept a puppy for herself and the dog has simply matured in an unexpected way, chances are that the dog is still quite exceptional. Just because a dog isn't show-worthy or skillful enough for police K-9 work doesn't mean that the dog won't make a fantastic companion. Most reputable breeders with adult dogs to sell will have made sure the dogs are well socialized, housebroken, and basically trained. The breeder will likely require that the dog be altered, but beyond that, the dog can become a great pet without the need for much rehabilitation.

Alert!

Always ask why a breeder is selling an adult dog. On occasion, a dishonest breeder may be trying to unload a dog with issues. Puppy mills will sell or auction off breeding females that are past their prime. These dogs often have had no socialization and have spent their lives in cages. Many could be beyond rehabilitation, so instead of buying the dog, report the breeder to your local police department or animal control officer.

Another possible source for a great German shepherd is a service dog agency, which trains dogs to serve the blind, those with hearing impairments, and people with impaired mobility. Many of these organizations have their own breeding programs for German shepherds. The puppies are raised by foster "puppy parents" to eighteen months of age. At this point, these dogs are evaluated for service training.

Not all dogs make it through service dog training. When this happens, the agency places the dog in a home. The puppy's foster parent has first dibs on purchasing the dog. If she declines, then the dog is available for adoption. Service agencies maintain a list of carefully screened individuals who would like to adopt any dog that fails the program. If you are interested and don't mind waiting—possibly for several years—you could wind up with one fantastic dog.

Working with a Breed Rescue

One of the best organizations through which to find a good, adoptable German shepherd is a German shepherd breed rescue. Breed rescues are national, regional, or local organizations that specialize in only one breed. They are comprised of experienced breeders, trainers, and owners of that breed. These people know everything about the breed and are great at evaluating dogs and matching dogs and owners based on compatibility.

If you are adopting an adult German shepherd through a breed rescue, you will have to endure a certain amount of screening. It may seem to be almost an invasion of privacy; however, rescues have to be extremely careful in selecting potential adopters. They want a rescued dog's adoptive home to be a permanent one, and they want new owners to be happy with the dogs they adopt.

The first thing you have to do is fill out a detailed application to adopt a rescued dog. The rescue will want to know such things as your experience with dogs, your past dogs' causes of death (did they live to a ripe old age or did they run away, never to be seen again?), the number and ages of any children in the home, what other pets are in the home, the size of your house and yard, and what your expectations are for your new shepherd.

 Fact

Some breed rescues are independent; others are members of a large network of rescue groups. Many breed rescues network with each other to help place dogs, provide long-distance transportation, and share training and behavioral advice.

After you have turned in your application, you will receive a call from one of the rescue volunteers. This person will answer any questions you might have and ask you for additional information.

 **Essential**

People have attempted to adopt rescue dogs for laboratory use, as bait for pit-fighting dogs, and for other unseemly operations. To this end, these phonies have also gone to such extremes as posing as a married couple or parents looking for a good family dog. It's no wonder rescues have to be careful.

If you pass the test up to this point, you'll be invited to meet some adult German shepherds. Either you'll be invited to one of the volunteer's homes to visit with dogs, or a volunteer may bring the dogs to your home. In addition to being able to talk to you in person, the volunteer wants to see how you react to the dogs. If you are preoccupied with picking hairs off your slacks or if your child runs screaming away from the dog, the volunteer will likely judge that you are not a good candidate for a shepherd rescue at this time.

Once you've been accepted to receive a rescue dog, you'll be placed on a waiting list. When the rescue receives a dog they think might be a match for you, they'll give you a call. Rescues try to make the best possible placements. If it looks like a particular dog may not adapt well to your lifestyle, or if he has issues that may be difficult for you to deal with, the rescue will wait until a more appropriate dog becomes available.

When you are finally introduced to the dog the rescue chooses for you, he will have been examined, received his vaccinations, and undergone tests for heartworm. The dog will have been in a foster home for at least ten days to a month, and his temperament will have been fully evaluated. It is likely, too, that the dog will be housetrained. Additionally, the dog will have received some obedience training and leash-walking skills.

Even if you've met all the criteria for adoption and you like the dog selected for you, the rescue still might not let you adopt this particular German shepherd. The reason for this is simple: Most rescues believe that it is not a true match until the dog chooses you. The rescue volunteer will be able to sense whether the dog feels comfortable with you.

Essential

The breed rescue from which you obtain your dog will be a lifelong source of information and assistance. You will find that these people are always willing to answer your questions and to assist you and your dog in any way possible.

After your new dog has chosen you, you will be asked to complete some paperwork. This will include a contract that allows the rescue to check up on the condition of the rescued dog at any time. The contract will also reserve the rescue group's right to take the dog back if he is found at any time to be neglected or abused. Additionally, the rescue will require you to return the dog if you can no longer take care of him for any reason.

How Shelters and Pounds Operate

Shelters and animal-control facilities (usually called "the pound") run the gamut from large, privately funded organizations with animal behaviorists and noted trainers on staff to municipally funded, understaffed facilities that are stretched to the limit. If you are fortunate and have an excellent shelter in your area, it is possible to work with the staff to find a good adult shepherd to adopt. If your local shelter doesn't have this volunteer or paid support, it will be much more difficult to find an adoptable German shepherd.

Municipally funded animal-control facilities pick up stray dogs and place them in holding areas with all other dogs that were found on that date. If a dog has no identification and is not claimed or adopted within a specified number of days, the dog is euthanized. Because of limited resources, pounds usually do not have placement services to help you evaluate a dog's health or temperament. Additionally, because of human rights issues, pounds often are not allowed to screen potential adopters; anyone who can pay the adoption price can claim a dog.

Unfortunately, the shepherd's biggest problem in a pound— even a good pound—is that they don't kennel well. For some shepherds, the noise of other dogs barking, the constant movement of strangers, and the lack of human interaction can cause stress. This can cause even a nice shepherd to appear off-kilter, extremely aggressive, or excessively timid.

It is virtually impossible to accurately assess a dog under these conditions. Even experts say they can't tell anything about a dog until he is in a quieter environment. For these reasons, you should not adopt a German shepherd from a shelter or pound unless you have experienced professional help.

Selecting an Adult Dog

What if a shelter or pound does not have a behaviorist on staff to help you find and evaluate a dog? In this case, you might look to a professional trainer who works with German shepherds, an experienced German shepherd breeder, a volunteer from a breed rescue, or a veterinarian with a specialty in behavior. You can expect to pay a fee for this expert's assistance; however, it's worth it to know that you're getting a good dog instead of one with health or temperament issues.

As you locate dogs that you're interested in, talk to every shelter volunteer you can find who has worked with and handled these dogs. Ask for their opinions about each dog's type. If a shepherd has managed to impress you and the shelter workers despite having lived in such a chaotic environment, it's probable that this dog will adjust well to any environment—including your home.

If you hear negative remarks from the volunteers, keep in mind that many shepherds are automatically labeled vicious or dangerous, when in actuality their behavior is frequently a reflection of the stressful surroundings. This is where a professional's guidance comes in; this person will be able to assess the dog's true potential.

◄ **Older dogs are just as fun as younger ones.**

Essential

Watch the dog you are interested in for lameness (favoring a hip or leg) or signs of past injuries. Poor coat condition and low body weight are usually superficial flaws—more often than not, these can be corrected with good nutrition, flea and tick medication, and a lot of love and care.

While at the shelter, you'll also want to read the explanation from the surrendering owner of the dog's likes, dislikes, and history with people. (An animal control facility won't have this information since the majority of their dogs are strays.) Again, when reading this document, take whatever the owner has written with a grain of salt. As awful as this may sound, owners frequently claim their dogs are aggressive toward children, can't be housebroken, or have any of a myriad of other faults to feel justified in dumping their dogs. Then again, the claims might be true. The only way to be fully sure is to have your expert thoroughly evaluate the dog's temperament.

Evaluating Temperament

The first thing your expert will want to do is move the dog to a quiet area. While in this area, it is important to allow the German shepherd to approach you on her own terms. You do not want to make a move to pat the dog or even make eye contact (which can be seen as a threatening gesture) until she has shown interest in you.

To begin, you and your shepherd expert should basically ignore the dog. The more approachable and less confrontational you appear, the faster the dog will warm up to you and begin to trust you. Remember, you know literally nothing of this dog's past or how people have treated her. Allow the dog to sniff you and even lick you. Make any movements slowly and in a nonthreatening way, keeping hands and arms low and not raised above the dog.

If the dog is warming up nicely to you and your expert and seems to have gotten comfortable with her surroundings, see if she shows any interest in playing with a ball or another toy. As she continues to relax and gain confidence, your expert may be able to handle her and test her tolerance for minimal contact. At this point, if all is going well, your expert will want to leash the dog and walk around the enclosure or take on extended walk outside of the facility, if possible. Using treats and a reassuring voice, your expert may work on a few simple obedience skills to see if the dog is willing to heed a handler.

The dog that is obviously friendly, loves handling, and trusts quickly is probably a good choice. Dogs that remain fearful and shy away from you or overreact to even the slightest movements or sounds are harder to evaluate. It could be that the dog is too damaged to be rehabilitated, or it could be that time away from the shelter with an experienced handler might be all the dog needs to blossom.

 Alert!

Generally, what you see at the shelter in terms of temperament will be the dog in her worst state. The moment she is out of the noisy surroundings, she will improve dramatically. On occasion, it is possible for an emaciated or very ill dog to appear complacent simply because she has so little energy and, as her health improves, to become domineering and aggressive.

Regardless, it is dangerous to take a chance on a dog that doesn't show improvement. If your expert feels that the distressed shepherd might warm up over time, you might consider making daily visits with the dog and observing if there's any change in the dog's attitude toward you. Of course, if there is any doubt in your expert's mind—or yours—as to the temperament of the shepherd, don't adopt her. As tough as it might be to walk away from a dog that will likely be euthanized, you can't risk it. Save your heart and home for the German shepherd that lavishes you with love and attention and pleads with you to take her home and keep her forever. This is the one you want.

Health

Virtually all German shepherds that wind up in shelters or pounds have not been treated with heartworm preventive. Consequently, many of these dogs have heartworms. The good news is that depending on the severity of the infestation and the overall health of the dog, most dogs can be treated for heartworm successfully.

Most abandoned or stray dogs have one or more types of intestinal worms. It is assumed, too, that strays and dumped dogs have not received any vaccinations. Shelters routinely vaccinate and worm dogs as they are accepted into their facilities; pounds do not. Depending on where you find your dog, you may need to take care of this with your veterinarian immediately.

 **Fact**

> If a German shepherd is two years old or older and not showing any clinical (physical) signs of elbow or hip dysplasia, the dog is probably okay and doesn't need to be X-rayed. You won't be breeding this dog, so no further testing is needed unless the dog begins to have soreness, lameness, or tenderness in his joints.

Many dogs coming into shelters and pounds are infested with fleas and ticks. Both types of facility will normally treat the dogs to rid them of these pests; however, what remains may be a scabby, inflamed, and infected mess. Unless the dog has a terrible skin allergy or another chronic condition, this problem will clear up with prompt veterinary care in a matter of time.

The Age Issue

Many people interested in adopting a dog are concerned with the dog's age for two main reasons. They are worried that an adult dog won't bond as deeply as a puppy, and they know that an adult dog won't live as long as a puppy.

As for the bonding issue, here are a couple of thoughts. Many of the dogs that are given up or found as strays have never had the opportunity to bond with a kind human being. They are still waiting for special people to come into their lives. When they find "their" people, these dogs bond quickly and intensely. Dogs that were well treated and have bonded with previous owners are also quite capable of bonding closely again.

As for the number of years that you will be able to enjoy your shepherd, it's important to remember that there are no guarantees in life. A puppy could be found to suffer from an unseen heart condition only months after entering your home and heart. An adolescent dog could get hit by a car. A middle-aged shepherd could get bone cancer. On the other hand, your puppy or adult shepherd could be with you for twelve years of quality companionship. Fear of eventually losing your dog is no reason not to adopt one. Adult dogs need loving homes just as much, if not more, than puppies do. Puppies are generally easier to adopt out, as their natural cuteness attracts owners.

In fact, there is one German shepherd that routinely gets passed up for adoption at breed rescues, as well as shelters and pounds: the senior dog. Often, the senior dog is one that has been a well-cared-for and loving pet. Her only fault may have been outliving her owner, or she may have been too large to follow her owner to an assisted-care facility. It is heartbreaking enough to think that a beloved dog can't be with her owner, and it's worse knowing that this dog may sit forever waiting for an owner at a rescue.

Preparing for Your New Dog

THE GERMAN SHEPHERD IS A HIGHLY inquisitive dog that will be interested in every area of your home and yard. For this reason, it is important to stay one step ahead of your puppy or dog by removing any potentially dangerous objects or materials before you bring the dog home.

In the Home

As intelligent as your shepherd is, he doesn't know which things are safe for him to ingest or touch and which are poisonous or unsafe. You will have to make sure that your German shepherd does not have access to anything you wouldn't give to him yourself. By puppy- or dog-proofing your home, you will keep your shepherd safe and protect your belongings from damage.

The strategies behind baby-proofing and shepherd-proofing a house are basically the same. The goal is to keep certain items out of sight and out of reach. When the shepherd is young, he will not be able to reach many items that are placed higher up; however, as your puppy matures, he will show extraordinary jumping abilities. As a general rule, you'll want to keep your tabletops and counters clear of breakables and clutter and free of food items.

Also, be aware that simply keeping items out of reach and out of sight may not be enough. This breed is known for its ability to figure out complex problems, particularly if there is a reward involved, such as food or gaining access to a favorite toy.

Your Shepherd's Own Space

Whether you are bringing home a puppy or a rescued adult, you will need to provide a place just for your German shepherd. The best way to do this is to set up a crate in a busy area of the home, such as the kitchen, family room, or home office. Your shepherd will want to have a safe cubby to retreat to but will not want to be left out of any of your activities.

Though your shepherd will want to be where the action is, he will also need to be kept safe and secure. Usually this means creating an area that can be sectioned off from the rest of the house with doors or baby gates. You will want your shepherd to be able to spend time with you without having to keep an eye on him at all times, particularly during the housetraining phase.

 Alert!

Shepherds have been seen spreading their front toes and using their paws very much like hands to open drawers and cabinet doors and to wiggle locking devices, like bolts and latches. Take this skill into consideration when deciding on your dog's space and also pay attention to what the shepherd might find in the drawers or cabinets.

The shepherd's area should also be in a part of your house with very few valuables, breakables, or toxic substances. Additionally, the area should be easy to clean in case of any accidents. Rooms that have hard floors, such as tile, linoleum, vinyl, or high-grade laminate floors, are all excellent choices. This type of floor will also teach your shepherd how to navigate on slick surfaces.

Food Storage and Eating Areas

Many of the food items that you eat regularly can be harmful to your dog. For example, onions are toxic to dogs, as are grapes and raisins, alcohol, tea and coffee, and chocolate. Dogs have different digestive systems than human beings do, and for reasons that are not always understood, they cannot process certain foods. Chocolate is probably the best-known example, but grapes and raisins are potentially lethal as well—even in small amounts, they have the power to cause renal (kidney) failure in a dog.

 **Essential**

Airtight containers used to store rice, cereals, dry noodles, and other such goods may keep bugs and mice out, but don't assume they will keep your shepherd from opening them. In fact, your shepherd may find that the plastic containers are nice chew toys. The lesson here is to keep the pantry door shut!

It takes only a few seconds for a shepherd to break into a sack of onions or a package of chocolate. Items as innocuous as potatoes can also pose a threat. Potatoes can be tempting to dogs of all ages, but if they are green-skinned or sprouting, they contain an alkaloid that can cause stomach and/or intestinal upset. Make sure the pantry door is secured at all times, and keep toxic food items safely stowed in containers with lids on high shelves.

Many people store their cleaning items under the sink in the kitchen. These abrasive cleansers, many of which contain bleach, can be very dangerous to your dog. A curious puppy or adult shepherd might gain access to this storage area unless you keep it tightly secured with a safety lock or other device. Even if you don't think your dog will try to get into this area, keep it locked as a precaution.

Another big problem for dog owners can be the garbage. Many people use a variety of methods to keep dogs from getting into the garbage can. Some squirt the dog with a water gun, others shake a can with a few pennies in it, and some people put a "scat mat" (a mat that gives an electric shock when stepped on) in front of the garbage can. However, there's a much simpler answer: to put the garbage can behind closed doors. The dog will not even be tempted if the can is completely out of sight.

Bathrooms and Laundry Facilities

The bathroom is another area of the house in which cleaners are routinely stored behind cabinet doors. Other poisonous items commonly kept under the sink or in cabinets include medication, soap, cosmetics, perfume, deodorant, shampoo, hair dye, toothpaste, and other personal-care products. Unless you can guarantee that you and your family members will always shut the bathroom door, you should put all these items behind cabinet doors and use child safety locks to secure them.

Another danger in the bathroom is the type of toilet-bowl cleaner that fastens onto the inside of the bowl and releases cleaner with every flush. If you use this type of product in your bathrooms, make sure that your shepherd will not be able to get to the toilet water or be able to remove and ingest the dispenser unit.

Alert!

Childproof lids on medications are not shepherd-proof. A puppy or adult dog can easily crack the plastic between his teeth and gain access to the materials inside. To prevent this, keep all medications locked up tightly.

In the area of your home where laundry facilities and products are kept, a shepherd can do a lot of damage. Soap, detergents, stain removers, bleach, ammonia, and other products are very toxic, even in small quantities. Additionally, even if your shepherd doesn't eat the product, spilling some of these products on his coat or splashing them in his eyes can be tragic. Keep these items away from your shepherd. If he does splash a product on himself, flush the area with water and call your veterinarian for advice on your way to an emergency clinic.

It is also important to keep clothing out of your German shepherd's reach. Any garments with loose straps, drawstrings, lace, buttons, or other details are likely to attract your dog's attention. Your shepherd, especially a puppy that likes to chew, will turn these garments into rags in no time. Garments that begin to unravel and expose loose strings and pieces of yarn can also pose a serious danger to canine chewers. Puppies and dogs can choke on long strands if they try to swallow them. Keeping your laundry out of sight will help protect your clothing and your dog.

Other Living Spaces

Almost every area of the house includes items that could be harmful to your dog. One of the most overlooked dangers that can be found in almost every room is electrical cords. Chewing through a lamp cord or a computer cable can potentially give a puppy or adult dog a lethal electrical jolt. If the shepherd chews partially through the cord when the item is not turned on or plugged in, the situation can become a fire hazard when power is restored to the object. As a preventative measure, cover cords and cables with protective plastic designed for this purpose or make sure the cords are completely hidden behind furniture or under rugs.

Other dangerous items include plug-in air fresheners. Not only could your shepherd get a shock by licking or trying to pull this item out of the socket, but eating the toxic chemicals in the plug-in is also hazardous. Dogs are also attracted to scented potpourri and candles. Ingestion of these items could cause serious illness, not to mention danger to the home if a candle is lit.

Your home office can pose a variety of hazards. Dropped staples, push pins, and paper clips are items that a shepherd might try to eat, thus cutting up his mouth, or to swallow, potentially causing extensive internal damage. Keep these items in drawers and make sure the floor is clear at all times. Also, make sure your office trashcan is not accessible to your shepherd.

Question?

Is it dangerous for your shepherd to eat "snacks" out of the cat's litter box?
The danger is not so much in the fecal matter itself but in the litter. Some litters contain chemicals to control odors and bacteria, which your shepherd would ingest if he picks anything out of the cat's box. Keep the litter box in an area that makes it easy for your cat to access it but not your shepherd.

If you have an insect or rodent problem in your home, be very careful about the chemicals you use to treat the situation. Ant killer, mouse poison, and roach motels are highly toxic. They also seem to be irresistible to dogs of all ages, perhaps because of their sweet odor or taste. Do not set out any bait in areas where your shepherd can get to them. Keep in mind that the shepherd is physically strong and even stronger willed. She will move filing cabinets and furniture to get to something she finds interesting.

Batteries can also be tempting chew items, and they are poisonous. Dispose of all sizes of spent batteries appropriately. Keep fresh batteries in closed drawers. If you keep nine-volt or larger batteries, remember that these will give your dog quite a jolt if he tries to chew on them. And be sure to put away items that contain batteries, such as remote controls and battery-powered portable radios and CD players.

Closets and Kids' Rooms

There are lots of things in your closets that your shepherd could find and chew on. Shoes, clothing, linens, and stored items like photos are prime candidates for your dog's unwanted attention. Most of these items aren't dangerous for the shepherd (except for the possibility of choking); however, the damage can cost you a small fortune—or it can cost you your memories. To avoid these problems, simply keep the closet door closed, as well as the door to the bedroom. Don't store anything poisonous (such as mothballs) in the closet either, just in case your shepherd figures out a way to get in.

Children's rooms also contain a variety of items that your shepherd would love to access. The only thing a German shepherd may love more than the kids themselves are the toys that they play with and conveniently leave strewn around the room. A kid's room is a chewing wonderland. Action figures and dolls with small parts can present choking hazards; children's art supplies, like markers, crayons, and paints can make a dog sick (and create quite a mess); and breakable items can leave shards of plastic or glass on the floor or in the carpet if tampered with. The good news is that children may be more motivated to pick up their toys if they know that the dog could get into them, but keep the bedroom doors closed as a precaution anyway.

Odds and Ends

Dogs of all breeds seem to be attracted to wooden items, such as windowsills, chair legs, table legs, and cabinet corners, to name a few. To prevent even the first gnaw mark on your furniture, cabinetry, and windows, consider using Bitter Apple spray or gel, or another foul-tasting, nontoxic product specifically designed for this purpose. Hopefully, your shepherd will be repelled by the first taste and learn that these areas are off-limits. These sprays can also be effective on pillows, hand towels, and other items a dog might steal for chewing.

Don't forget to check your home for plants that are toxic, too. Aloe vera, amaryllis, azalea, chrysanthemum, cyclamen, Dieffenbachia, English ivy, hydrangea, Kaffir lily, philodendron, and poinsettia are just a few plants commonly found in homes that can cause anything from minor irritation to severe illness in dogs. Keep these plants (and any nontoxic plants you don't want your shepherd to "prune") out of reach or outside of the home.

Garage

The garage presents two different kinds of probable hazards to your shepherd: heavy and/or sharp objects, and poisons. If your garage is like most, it is probably chock-full of items, from tools and automotive equipment to lawnmowers and painting supplies. The objects that are most dangerous to your puppy or adult shepherd are likely within easy sight and reach, making the hazards even more prominent.

Falling Objects

If your shepherd is investigating your garage, she's not going to realize that your ladder is leaning a bit precariously against the wall. She also won't notice that the shelving, which she's thinking of climbing in her quest to get that paintbrush, is not sturdy and can't support her weight. Nor does she realize that tugging on an oily cloth on the shelf is going to send several paint cans flying. Even just walking around in the garage can send a row of bikes tumbling, which can cause harm to both the bikes and the dog.

Puppies are most susceptible to injury from falling objects, but adult shepherds are not completely safe either. The best way to avoid trouble in the garage is to keep the area tightly secured and to make sure the dog has no reason to enter. If she should get in, at least be sure that all items in your garage are safely stowed out of reach.

Other Dangers

Most people are aware that antifreeze is a very toxic substance. Even a few drops lapped up by a wandering dog can be lethal. There are many other dangerous items in the garage as well:

- Leftover paint
- Fertilizer
- Insecticide
- Weed killer
- Rat poison
- Oil
- Transmission fluid
- Wax and polish
- Nails, screws, and other sharp objects

Again, the best way to avoid disaster is to keep the dog out of the garage at all times. However, if she (or a child, for that matter) should wander into the garage, you want to be sure that all dangerous items are tightly secured in boxes, crates, cans, or jugs with lids. As an added bonus, your clean, organized garage will be much more user-friendly.

Outside Areas

Once you've shepherd-proofed your home, you'll also need to check the surrounding outdoor property for hazardous material. Just as you did inside, you should be sure there are no exposed electrical wires, cords, or cables on the exterior of your home. It is also good to know what kinds of paints have been used on the exterior of your home. Remember, lead-based paints can cause a lot of damage to dogs with chewing habits.

▲ **Make sure your German shepherd gets plenty of exercise!**

Other dangers include stairs or walkways in disrepair, benches or statues that could be knocked over by an enthusiastic shepherd, and large equipment, such as lawnmowers, that a dog could collide with. If a shepherd mistakes a glass door for negative space, he might run right through it. Likewise, mesh screens used to keep flying insects out of a porch or patio will not deter a shepherd running at full speed. The best thing to do in these cases is acquaint your shepherd with glass doors and screens so that he knows they are solid dividers. Once he learns that the door must be opened to allow passage, he will remember not to run straight through.

Fencing

A fenced backyard is an absolute must if you have a German shepherd. This breed should never be chained up outside; the shepherd has far too much energy to be trapped in one spot. A shepherd could become dangerously aggressive if kept this way—one third of all fatal dog attacks involve a chained dog. The dog must be free to run and play within a defined area so that you can keep track of the dog while he expends his energy. Statistically, a chained dog is one of the most frequent causes of serious bites, attacks, and fatalities. If you don't already have a fence for your yard, put one up before you get the dog. Be sure the fence is sturdy and tall enough that the shepherd cannot jump over it.

 **Essential**

If your shepherd turns out to be an escape artist, you might consider resetting your fence. Some owners have had great success in discouraging climbers and jumpers by adjusting the panels of the fence to make them slope inwards slightly at the top, so they lean into the yard.

If you already have a fence, survey it for hazards. With a wooden fence, make sure each section is securely nailed or screwed to the posts. The sections should not be wobbly, and they should be nailed on the inside of the posts. If the fencing is on the outside of the posts (the posts are in your yard), your shepherd might be able to push the fence section outward and get loose. Also, be sure that no nails, screws, or splinters are protruding from the fence. Areas with rotted wood should also be replaced. Sand any rough areas or peeling paint so that the dog isn't tempted to chew or scratch. Finally, be sure that the fence is low enough to the ground that the dog can't crawl beneath it.

Chain-link fences should also be inspected for any signs of metal failure. The fence should be tight between its metal posts and sunk into the ground. Shepherds *can* climb chain-link fences. Usually they won't do this if they are receiving enough exercise, mental stimulation, and interaction with their owners; however, there are always exceptions. You might also consider adding a below-ground invisible electric fence that works with a companion collar to alert the dog when he is approaching the fence and physically discourage him from violating the barrier.

Lawn and Garden

Many ornamental plants and virtually all spring and summer bulbs are toxic. Be aware of which plants in your yard are hazardous, and either pull them up and replant them elsewhere or make it so that your shepherd can't gnaw or eat them. If you're hesitant about taking any such drastic measures, make sure you're always outside with your shepherd. Keep an eye on him, and note whether he shows any interest in these plants. If he does, either supervise him heavily or move the plants. Some poisonous plants that are commonly found in yards include the following:

- Azaleas
- Baneberry
- Lantana
- Chokecherry
- Daffodil, hyacinth, and tulip bulbs
- Foxglove
- Hydrangea
- Oleander
- Wisteria
- Yew

Of course, the plants you grow aren't the only dangers to your dog in your yard. The fertilizers, insecticides, and weed killers you use are also hazardous. Before using any chemicals in your yard or on your lawn, read the labels very carefully. Some products are no longer toxic after they dry, while others remain toxic in any form.

If in doubt, don't use the product. Investigate other methods of eradicating pests, such as using an insecticidal soap that is harmless to animals—and to you. Your German shepherd is certainly more important than a pristine garden and perfect lawn. Don't forget that you can always fence off areas of your yard that you don't want your shepherd to enter. If you're creative, you can make this part of your landscape design and have the best of both worlds.

CHAPTER 7

Bringing Your Shepherd Home

THE DAY IS QUICKLY APPROACHING when you will finally be able to bring home your new German shepherd. Whether you are adopting an adult dog or purchasing a puppy, you have several preparations to make for your new canine.

Supplies to Have on Hand

Bringing home a new dog is a big event. In the excitement, it is not uncommon for new owners to forget to purchase all the supplies they will need when the shepherd arrives. Among the most critical items are food, bowls for food and water, a collar, and a leash. You'll also want several safe chew toys, as well as supplies to clean (and clean up after) your shepherd. And, of course, there's the crate and all the supplies that go with this purchase.

Food and Bowls

Your new dog will need to eat only a few hours after you bring him home, so be sure to have food and bowls on hand. Not just any food will do. Ask your breeder (or the shelter/rescue staff, if adopting) what food your dog is currently eating and how much he eats at each meal. Whether or not you plan to continue with this food, you shouldn't introduce a new food immediately—this could cause gastrointestinal problems. For more information on how to gradually introduce a new food, see Chapter 9.

ᴖ Fact

Sometimes a breeder may not be sure how much an individual puppy eats if a communal puppy bowl is used. To make sure you are feeding your puppy enough, measure dry commercial food into a bowl and give the puppy thirty minutes to eat. After this time, pick up the bowl and measure how much he ate. This will give you a good idea of how much to feed him regularly.

When it comes to choosing food and water bowls for your new shepherd, keep in mind that puppies and some adult dogs take great pleasure in carrying their bowls around, stepping in them and tossing the food, or chewing on them. Plastic bowls are inexpensive, but they can be easily tipped and destroyed and are difficult to clean. Ceramic bowls are heavy enough to be stable, but they break easily and are often not dishwasher safe. Stainless steel bowls are easy to clean and relatively durable, and bottom-weighted bowls won't tip.

Collars

You'll need to know what size collar your shepherd currently wears, so call your breeder or the shelter/rescue to find out your dog's size. Otherwise you can measure the dog's neck, making sure that you allow room for comfort without making it too loose. Next, you must decide what kind of collar to purchase. A flat-buckle collar is a good choice for a puppy or an adult, as this collar type is often used for early puppy training. However, a young puppy can grow through several sizes before he reaches maturity.

Alert!

Collars are frequently made of nylon web, cotton, or leather. Nylon is sturdy, but it can rub the hair off a dog's neck. Flat cotton collars can be comfortable and decorative although they usually aren't very durable. Leather is an excellent material for a collar. It's durable, and rolled leather won't rub, but it's often more expensive than other materials.

An adjustable collar can last longer as your puppy grows, but it is a little more dangerous. When the collar is at its tightest adjustment, it leaves a significant amount of collar to be tucked, forming a loop. An active puppy can get this loop hung up on his crate or outside on the fence. Additionally, the adjustable collar typically fastens with a plastic clip. Some of these clips are much more durable than others, so make sure that you don't buy one that will break easily.

Training or choke collars are made either of rolled nylon or leather (like a rope) or metal links. The collar is made to tighten, or choke, as the dog pulls. You may choose to use this collar for training purposes, but it should not be used as your shepherd's everyday collar. This collar is easily caught on protruding objects and could potentially strangle your shepherd.

Leashes

Leashes come in varying thicknesses, lengths, and materials. If you are purchasing a puppy, choose a lightweight leash with a small clip. Owners frequently make the mistake of running out and purchasing the thickest, longest leash available. A thick leash has a heavy clip, which will clunk against your puppy's head. As your puppy grows, you can increase the weight of the leash (and clip) accordingly.

Leashes come in an assortment of materials: nylon web, cotton, leather, and chain (of metal links). It is not wise to purchase a chain leash for your shepherd. Though this leash is durable, it looks tough and gives the wrong impression. You do not want people to think that your shepherd is mean, fierce, and ready to attack. German shepherds are already feared by much of the general public; you don't need to add to this impression.

A better leash to choose is one made of leather because it is durable, lightweight, and strong. The only drawbacks are price and taste. Leather is more expensive than nylon web or cotton, and some dogs find leather irresistible as a chew toy. Nylon web can be tough on the hands if you have to reel a dog in, and cotton must be cleaned more often and tends to wear on the edges.

Chews and Toys

You can't spoil a puppy or dog with too many toys or chew items at once. Many trainers recommend that you keep about twenty items on hand but only offer the dog a few of these at any given time. This way, you can rotate the chews and toys and create the element of surprise. Dogs are very much like children. If they haven't seen a toy or chew for a few days, its reappearance is treated like a special event. If you have many items for your shepherd, keep roughly half of them out and the rest hidden in a cupboard. Every day, replace four items that have been out with four items that were hidden.

The toys and chews you select should all be shepherd-safe. Puppies and adults have strong bites and can break a rawhide bone into chunks or tear a weaker rubber toy easily. Unfortunately, the smaller chunks or torn pieces can become choking hazards. When selecting these items, look for things like knotted rope toys, sturdy tug toys, tough rubber shapes that can be stuffed with dog biscuits, and extra-large tennis balls that are too big for a shepherd to swallow.

Cleaning Strategies and Supplies

Even if your shepherd is coming from a reputable breeder or rescue, you may still want to bathe your puppy or dog before allowing him into your home. Make sure you use a shampoo that is tear-free and designed specifically for dogs. Shampoos made for humans may be too abrasive or too difficult to rinse out of the dog's coat.

Many shepherds have very sensitive skin and/or skin allergies. You may need to purchase a medicated shampoo from your veterinarian if this is the case. If you're not sure whether your shepherd has a skin problem, use an oatmeal-based canine shampoo that is made for sensitive or allergic dogs.

If your dog is not yet housetrained, you must be ready to deal with a few accidents. You should be prepared to spot-clean your floors and carpet with a supply of paper towels, stain remover, and an enzyme-eating cleaner. Several products are specifically made to break down the chemicals in dog urine so that the wet spot no longer has odor. Stain removers can be very helpful, but make sure you test yours on a hidden area first. If the product does not discolor your carpet or upholstery, it is safe to use in the future.

Purchasing a Crate

In the last few years, the crate-and-carrier market has expanded greatly with the addition of many new and innovative products. From side-loading metal wire crates and pop-up tentlike mesh crates to collapsible and partitioned kennels, there is a crate out there for every dog and every budget.

Wire Crates

The German shepherd loves to be able to see what is going on around her. The wire crate enables your puppy or dog to see her surroundings even when she's spending time in her special space. The metal wire crate provides the best air circulation possible when traveling by car, too, and thanks to the removable metal tray at the bottom, this crate can be completely and thoroughly cleaned.

 **Essential**

Wire crates can come with convenient features, such as a partition that can be moved within the crate to accommodate a growing shepherd from puppyhood to adulthood. Other crates are made to fit sideways in the rear of an SUV or station wagon. These crates open both at the end and at the side. Metal crates are often collapsible for easy storage.

So what's the downside? Some shepherds prefer a more den-like kennel and are uneasy being exposed all the time. Other shepherds may have such severe separation anxiety that they will chew, twist, and rip escape holes in the crate, creating a very dangerous situation. The metal crate is not accepted for airline travel and can be quite heavy to carry. A quality metal crate is also relatively expensive—often $100 or more, not including a high-quality pad.

Hard-Shell Plastic Carriers

These plastic carriers come in two pieces, with a top and a bottom that fasten together. They are inexpensive, too; a good, airline-approved crate may cost as little as $25 for a puppy or $50 to $75 for an adult dog. Plastic carriers are lightweight and just about perfect for the puppy or dog that prefers a warm, cozy space.

The plastic crate does have a few shortcomings. For one, the crate cannot be partitioned. That means it will be necessary to purchase a smaller crate for a puppy and upgrade to a larger crate when your shepherd reaches adolescence. Additionally, the air circulation is not as good as that in a wire or mesh crate, and the crate doesn't break down into pieces that are easily stored or stowed away. Finally, because of the cracks and tiny fissures that occur in plastic, it is nearly impossible to completely clean and sterilize this crate.

Mesh Tents

Mesh crates set up like tents and are the ultimate in lightweight temporary housing. Mesh traveling crates are made with a screen-like material that is supported by PVC tubing. They collapse into very manageable sizes, have tremendous air circulation, and are nice options for a well-behaved, calm dog that is reliable and quiet in a crate.

For the majority of shepherds, this crate can only be used while the owner is supervising the dog. A shepherd—whether a pup or an adult—can rip through the mesh walls easily, if she is so inclined. The mesh kennel is also not safe for traveling in a car because it doesn't limit the dog's movement in the event of a sudden stop.

 Question?

How do I size a crate to fit my shepherd?
The general rule is that the crate should be just large enough for the puppy or adult to stand up without crouching, turn around easily, and lie down comfortably. If the crate is any larger, it makes house-training difficult.

A Head Start on Training

You already know the importance of beginning training with your shepherd as soon as possible. What you might not know is that early puppy training classes fill up very quickly. Unless you reserve a space before you bring your puppy home, you may find that you can't get into a class for months.

▲ Signing up for training early will benefit both you and your shepherd.

Be sure you scout out the training classes in your area. Choose one that supports a positive, reward-based training program and that does not use training or choke collars on puppies. Make a deposit to hold a spot in an appropriate, upcoming session, and mark the dates and times on your calendar.

Alert!

Your veterinarian will advise you not to put your puppy in contact with lots of other dogs until you've completed the full series of puppy vaccinations. These vaccinations should be administered when the puppy is between twelve and sixteen weeks of age. Ask your veterinarian when she feels your puppy can begin group lessons, as the relative danger of viruses can vary from region to region.

An adopted adult dog should begin training immediately. He won't be able to attend an early puppy class, but he should be enrolled in a beginning obedience class. You may find that your shepherd knows all of his commands and breezes through this class. That's fine; the experience is building his trust in you, as well as his self confidence. This also presents an opportunity for you to reward his good behavior and teach him what you expect of him on a daily basis.

Important Appointments

Before you pick up your puppy or rescued dog, you should make an appointment with your veterinarian to have your shepherd's health checked within twenty-four hours of bringing him home. A good breeder will provide a health guarantee for the puppy; however, you must have the puppy examined by a veterinarian within forty-eight to seventy-two hours for this guarantee to be valid and binding.

Another appointment you might want to make is with a groomer. Adopted or rescued dogs are often in need of a bath, possibly a flea-and-tick dip, a good brushing, and a nail clipping. Professional groomers are well equipped to deal with anxious, nervous dogs. Just be sure to apprise them of your adopted dog's temperament and experiences (if any) with water and a brush.

The Ride Home

The most important thing to remember to bring with you when you go to pick up your shepherd is a crate in which to bring her home. New owners often forget to bring a secure way of transporting the German shepherd. This can cause several problems.

With puppies, the ride home is possibly their first ride in a moving car. Puppies are known to have sensitive stomachs, and it doesn't take much motion to make them vomit. If the new puppy is in your lap when this happens, it can be a bit messy. If the puppy is in a crate, on the other hand, this is relatively easy to clean up.

Puppies can also be quite nervous and squirmy during the car ride and have been known to get themselves and their drivers in trouble. Accidents (and near accidents) have occurred when puppies have wriggled underneath the brake pedal, inadvertently hit the automatic window button, or knocked the gearshift into neutral.

Adult dogs should be brought home in a carrier for all the same reasons: ease of cleaning up after any accidents, limited distracting movements, and safety for the dog in case of a sudden stop or accident. But there's one more reason: Adult dogs have been known to act in unusual ways when in a strange car. In fact, perfectly well-tempered dogs have been known to panic to the point of biting the driver or a passenger in their rush to get out of the car. Play it safe, and keep the shepherd contained during the ride.

What You'll Need the First Night

Patience is the key ingredient to a successful first night with the dog at home. If you are bringing home a new puppy, don't plan to get a lot of sleep that night. (With any luck, you don't have to work the following morning.) This is your puppy's first night away from her mother and littermates, and the experience can be unnerving for any dog.

Your puppy will be used to sleeping in a warm, cozy puppy pile. Now she'll be alone in her crate. You can help her adjust by making sure she has a lot of warm, comfortable bedding. You might also consider wrapping a warm hot-water bottle in a towel and placing this in her crate, too.

Essential

Your puppy will find it very comforting to be close to you, but resist allowing a young pup to sleep with you. You may find that you don't wake up at the pup's request to go to the bathroom. Additionally, what might have seemed like a great idea when the puppy weighed only 5 or 10 pounds may not seem so great when he's full grown (around 60 pounds) and taking up half of a queen-size bed.

There is one more item that will help comfort your puppy on her first night with you. A female dog emits a specific hormone while caring for her puppies that the pups find comforting. In fact, research indicates that the scent of this hormone is comforting to a dog for the whole of her life. If you don't have an item with the mother's scent on it, consider purchasing a product that contains dog appeasing pheromone (DAP). These products usually come in the form of sprays and can be applied to your puppy's bedding.

Put your puppy's crate in your room so she can see and hear you. Close the door so that you know exactly where she is at all times. And don't worry—she'll let you know when she needs to relieve herself. Of course, it might be difficult to discern this request when her howling, crying, and barking could seem nearly continuous. Many owners find that cozying up next to the crate for the night and reaching into the crate to stroke the puppy is enough to help settle her.

Adult dogs are typically much quieter their first night home. Still, you might find that instead of crying or howling, your adopted dog pants, paces, or otherwise acts uncomfortable. As with the puppy, keep your shepherd's crate close to you in your bedroom. Your presence will be comforting to her. Also consider giving her a good chew toy to work on in her crate.

What's in a Name?

Have you thought of a call name for your shepherd? If you've pur- chased a puppy from a breeder, it is likely that the pup has already been named. Typically, the first word in the pup's registered name is the breeder's kennel name, after which another name follows. Breeders might have theme litters—with pups in a litter all named after German breweries, for example—or letter litters, in which puppies from the first litter have names that begin with A, the sec- ond litter with B, and so on. For example, the name "King's Alfie" is a combination of the kennel name (King) and a name that begins with A (Alfie) to denote a puppy from the breeder's first litter.

Esseñtial

If you are adopting a rescue shepherd and plan on applying for an indefinite listing privilege number, you can name your dog anything you want. However, you cannot give your dog a kennel name that is someone else's. Come up with something original and fitting to your unique dog.

Although your puppy may already have a registered name, you will still need to come up with a call name. You can give the pup a name that is related to his registered name, such as Sunny for King's Sunshine, or you can come up with something totally different, like Bud or Angel. Your puppy's call name is totally yours to create—just try to limit it to one or two distinct syllables. Long, complicated names are not easy to say in a hurry, nor are they easy for your shepherd to recognize.

CHAPTER 8

Life with a Rescued Adult

ONCE YOU BRING A RESCUED ADULT DOG into your home, your life is never the same. You will experience the indescribable feeling of saving a dog's life, bringing back his health, and restoring his faith and trust in humans. Though you can expect some challenges and frustrations along the way, your investment will be rewarded many times over.

The First Twenty-four Hours

If you've selected a dog from a good breed rescue or shelter, you can be assured that your new shepherd is very deserving of a loving, permanent home. These placement organizations simply do not place dogs unless they have excellent temperaments and are anticipated to do well in their new homes.

That said, it is important that you set even the best shepherd on the path to success. This means that you need to avoid situations in which your shepherd might become frightened, hurt, or threatened. This is particularly important during the first twenty-four hours that your adopted dog is home. During this period, she is not only adjusting to you as her new owner but also to the sights, scents, and sounds in your home—many of which she may never have experienced before.

Even if you had a professional accompany you to the shelter to evaluate your dog's temperament, you still won't be able to anticipate all of her reactions. If she is startled, will she cower, jump away, or respond with a bite? The rescue or shelter you worked with will tell you how the dog responded to many different stimuli, but these reactions could vary when she is in your home.

 **Essential**

Some rescued dogs walk into their new homes as if they've lived there all their lives. Others take longer to feel comfortable. How long your shepherd will take to adjust depends on his past life experiences, his overall temperament, and his trust in you. Equally important is your patience and understanding of his needs.

For example, a young rescued male was an absolute dream dog at his foster home. He loved everyone, tolerated the cats, and was quick to learn basic commands. It wasn't until the dog was placed in his adoptive home that his hot button was discovered. This rescue dog's hot button was ceiling fans; he would become frenzied when one was turned on in a room. Luckily, he was successfully moved to a new family's home (without a ceiling fan). It is idiosyncrasies such as these that can be difficult to predict.

The First Month

When you bring your rescued adult home, he will most likely appear nervous. He'll be panting, sniffing everything, and pacing or moving constantly. This can last for hours—though it might feel like days. To help him relax, limit his explorations to one room, using baby gates or doors to close off this room from the rest of the home. This will make it easier for him to search every single nook and cranny thoroughly, which he will do before he relaxes.

Additionally, confining him to one room allows you to keep an eye on him. This way, he can't get in trouble by having an accident somewhere in the home or grabbing a forbidden item to chew on.

Make sure that while your shepherd is checking out his new surroundings, he also has access to plenty of fresh water. Constant motion and panting can dehydrate a dog fairly quickly. Also, be cognizant of your shepherd's needs to relieve himself. High levels of stress or excitement can cause intestinal distress or overwhelming thirst. Also, you should have a variety of chew toys scattered about the floor to help keep him occupied.

Place his crate in this same room, with the door open so that he can retreat to his den when he feels tired or wants to be left alone. If he's hesitant about entering the crate, entice him to enter with a few tossed treats—leaving the door open. When he becomes more comfortable going in and out of the crate, toss the treats again. Once the shepherd is in the crate, give the command, "Go to your place." Soon your shepherd will learn that "Go to your place" means he should retire to his crate.

Esseñtial

If you have children, you must make sure that they know the dog's crate is absolutely off limits to them. Your shepherd needs her own space; no child should be allowed to crawl in the crate, reach into the crate to remove a toy, or even lean into the crate to pet the shepherd. The dog must feel secure in this space.

When you prepare to crate your shepherd for a significant time period (fifteen minutes or more) make sure to put a "busy" chew, such as a good knucklebone or hard, rubber toy stuffed with treats, in the crate for the dog. The chew or stuffed toy serves to keep the dog busy and entertained while you're gone. It also reinforces the notion that good things happen when she's in her crate.

You should also consider feeding your shepherd in his crate, at least for the first several days. This allows your shepherd to feel that his food is safe and that no one is going to take it away from him. Additionally, if he's eating his food in his crate, this eliminates the possibility of his acting inappropriately with you or your children—until you can determine his behavior around food and work on any issues he might have.

The First Night

An adult dog's first night at a new home is similar to the first night for a puppy. The adult rescue won't be pining for any littermates or for Mom; however, he may be unsettled. In particular, he may not want to be left alone. To help him feel more comfortable, keep his crate in your bedroom at night. He will find your presence reassuring.

Make sure your dog has comfortable, cozy bedding in his crate, too. Adult dogs are far less likely to soil their crates than puppies because they have the ability to control their bladders and bowels, even when nervous or stressed. The act of chewing can be calming to a dog. Be sure to give your shepherd a chew toy or bone so he has something to keep him busy.

Question?

Are there any holistic remedies that are safe to use to calm a shepherd?
One of the most frequently used holistic remedies for stressful situations is the Bach flower essence called Rescue Remedy. Flower essences are very pure extracts from flowers that are grown specifically for healing purposes. Each flower essence is believed to have a different, positive effect on an animal's emotions. The drops can be placed in the dog's water or rubbed on his gums.

Additionally, in anticipation of a sleepless first night, you might be interested in purchasing a product featuring dog appeasing pheromone (DAP) that you can attach to or place near your shepherd's crate. DAP mimics the unique scent of a specific hormone produced by lactating canine moms. A dog, no matter what age, recognizes and finds this hormone relaxing and comforting. DAP has shown promise in clinical trials and could be very helpful in settling your rescued shepherd.

Rescue Dogs and Kids

Shepherds can be great with children. If you have children, your German shepherd might very well take to them immediately; however, you shouldn't expect this to happen. In most cases, your new shepherd needs to bond with your children and learn to trust them, too. Your biggest job could be teaching your children to be kind and gentle with the new shepherd.

A young child doesn't have to be mean-spirited to poke a dog's eye, twist a tail, pull a whisker, or step on a toe; he could simply be curious or clumsy. Children also like to use dogs as pillows, to kiss their faces, and to touch their feet. These actions can cause a dog a lot of stress, especially when repeated often. Kids also react impulsively, which can unsettle a dog. If the dog is chewing on a child's toy, the child's first reaction is to grab the toy back. This could startle a shepherd and cause her to growl, bark, or even bite.

What this boils down to is that you must set your shepherd up for success by controlling your children around the dog at all times. To do this, you must continually remind your children of the rules pertaining to the dog. Some basic rules include the following:

- Do not pet the dog when she is eating.
- The dog is not a cushion or a horse; do not lean on her or try to ride her.
- Leave the dog alone when she is sleeping. Wake her by saying her name, not by touching her.

- Keep your face out of the dog's face.
- No running, screaming, or hitting each other in the home. The shepherd is likely to get involved in any conflicts.
- Never go in the dog's crate or poke your fingers inside. The dog is entitled to protect her space.
- Never try to take anything out of the dog's mouth. Ask a parent for help.

In addition to enforcing these rules, you must supervise the children when they are around the shepherd. If you can't supervise directly, you must be able to separate the dog from the children to prevent trouble.

Typical Problems

A shepherd that is adopted from a responsible breed rescue or a top-notch shelter usually doesn't exhibit serious problem behaviors. In other words, you won't have to worry about owning a dangerous dog. The problems that you will most likely encounter with your adopted shepherd will occur during the dog's initial adjustment to your home and family.

Stairs and Slick Floors

A dog that has spent his days in a backyard or in a single-story home is not necessarily going to be able to navigate a staircase, especially if there are gaps between the steps or it is made of slick material.

One way to help your dog overcome his fear of stairs is by working with him on shorter flights of steps, such as the longer, lower steps sometimes found in parks or public buildings. Often a shepherd can take this skill and transfer it to the steps in your home. If your shepherd is highly motivated by food, you can use treats to lure him up and down the stairs.

Many German shepherds also have difficulties navigating on slick floors. When you consider where these adopted dogs have come from, it makes sense. Many have never even seen the inside of a home and have spent all their time outside in the dirt, mud, or grass. The first time an inexperienced dog sets foot on a surface that is smooth and slick—and totally foreign to him—he may transform into a stiff-legged, wobbly mess. The dog could respond to the surface by frantically clawing at the floor for balance, which is not good for your dog or your floor.

 **Essential**

Physical and verbal corrections are not effective when dealing with a frightened dog and will only make him panic more on a slick floor. Don't verbally comfort the dog, either—he will interpret this coddling as a reward for fearing the floor. Instead, assist in regaining balance by gently steadying him.

One way to help your shepherd adjust to slick floors is to place rubber-backed rugs or bathmats in key places, such as entrances and exits of rooms, around corners, and at the top and bottom of steps leading in or out of rooms. These nonskid rugs will give your shepherd a chance to make a more calm and controlled entry into the room. As your shepherd gains more confidence with his balance and control on these slick floors, you can gradually reduce the number of rugs and mats.

Soft Spots and Phobias

Not knowing your shepherd's background puts you at a slight disadvantage in terms of sensitive spots on the dog's body. A rescued dog may look perfectly normal, but when touched in a specific place, he might yelp, jump away, snap, or even grab your hand.

With careful examination you might be able to find a scar from a pellet or bullet injury or another wound. However, there might not be any visible indication of harm. For example, it is not uncommon for a dog that has had an ear infection to wince or whimper when you touch the ear, even though the ear is no longer infected. A dog's natural reaction to pain or fear of pain is biting. Your shepherd will probably not react so strongly if he trusts you, but trust takes time to build. So, when grooming and handling your shepherd, be gentle, calm, and cautious as you learn more about your dog.

Other quirks your dog might have include phobias. You never know what might be scary to your new shepherd. It could be the sound of a vacuum cleaner, a plastic bag, or a train whistle. It could be the sight of a rolled newspaper, a hose, or a hairbrush. How you handle your shepherd when she is startled or frightened by an everyday sound or object will largely influence her next reaction to the same sound or item.

 **Fact**

A dog that is extremely stressed or anxious—or even extremely bored—may compulsively lick one spot on his body, creating a wound. If your dog is doing this, examine his environment carefully. Is there a noise, object, or person upsetting him? Do your best to eliminate the stressor and calm the dog.

The best thing to do when you notice that a certain sound or object upsets your dog is nothing—don't react. If your shepherd startles when you turn on the garbage disposal, ignore him. If you say, "Oh, it's okay, sweetie," and stroke and pat the dog, you are not comforting him. In actuality, you are rewarding his behavior, which will only prompt him to continue his phobia. If you ignore him when he responds inappropriately to something, he is much more likely to slowly become acquainted with the object. Only when your shepherd behaves appropriately is it okay to reward her with pats and treats.

Separation Anxiety

A very common problem with rescued German shepherds is separation anxiety. The severity of the situation can range from mild panting, whimpering, and clawing at the crate to full-blown clawing and breaking apart the crate to escape.

Still, it is very important that a dog with separation anxiety be crated, as she is likely to hurt herself and cause more damage if left loose in the home. Panicked dogs have broken through storm doors, clawed and chewed holes through drywall, ripped window blinds from their brackets, and shredded entire couches.

▲ Rescue dogs need extra time, patience, and love.

Separation anxiety is a behavior that can be lessened extensively through a variety of training methods (described in Chapter 13). These methods include keeping the shepherd active in an enjoyable activity while you're gone (such as working on a chew toy), acclimating the shepherd to her crate so she feels comfortable and safe, teaching the shepherd that you *will* return, and desensitizing her to cues that you are leaving (the jingle of keys, putting on coat, etc.).

Other Pets

Shepherds can get along fabulously with cats, as well as other household pets. You will find, however, that even if a shepherd comes to you with the reputation of being great with other pets, your dog will need to learn that the other animals in your home are pets and not prey.

Introduce your pets to the shepherd gradually, over time. Make sure the pet is safe and protected from the shepherd at all times. For example, if you have a pet rabbit, allow your shepherd to see the rabbit in its crate for brief periods of time, whether a few seconds or a few minutes, and reward the dog only for calm behavior. Make the introductory sessions very brief so that your shepherd has the greatest chance of success.

As the dog begins to accept the rabbit, have a family member hold the rabbit securely in his arms and allow the shepherd to gently investigate. If your shepherd appears to be disinterested in the pet, you might be able to briefly place it on the floor; however, be extremely careful. Your shepherd may not mean to hurt the rabbit, but he is large enough that even a playful swat could seriously injure or kill some small pets.

Where to Get Help

If you have any questions or concerns regarding your adopted shepherd, your first phone call should be to the breed rescue volunteer or shelter worker from whom you adopted your shepherd. This person will know your individual shepherd well and will have a reference point on which to base any advice. Additionally, particularly in the case of German shepherd breed rescues, this volunteer will be in tune with the shepherd breed and will know the challenges the breed can present and have some possible solutions to offer.

If the situation is more complex or the solutions you're offered by the rescue or shelter just aren't working, there are other resources you can turn to for help. These professionals include the following (details provided in Appendix A):

- *Veterinary behaviorist:* This individual not only holds a veterinary degree (DVM) but is also a diplomate, or board-certified specialist, of the American College of Veterinary Behaviorists (ACVB). To find a veterinary behaviorist, contact the American Veterinary Medical Association (AVMA).

- *Veterinary behavior consultant:* This individual is not board certified; however, he has in-depth knowledge of behavior, as well as behavior modification training and medical therapies. The AVMA can also be contacted for referrals to veterinary behavior consultants, as can the Animal Hospital Association of America.

- *Animal behaviorist:* The veterinary behaviorist might be called the psychiatrist of the canine world. The certified animal behaviorist—who holds a Ph.D. in animal behavior and is certified through the Animal Behavior Society (ABS)—would then be the psychologist. Unlike the veterinary behaviorist, the certified animal behaviorist cannot prescribe medications for your dog. Animal behaviorists can be located by contacting the ABS at the American Editorial Office for Animal Behavior.

- *Trainer:* To find an accomplished trainer who is good at solving behavioral challenges, contact your veterinarian, breed rescue, shelter, German shepherd breeder, and other canine-savvy individuals for referrals. You may also try contacting the Association of Pet Dog Trainers (APDT).

Building a Lifetime Bond

You may think that it will take months for your shepherd to begin to truly bond with you. In actuality, the bonding begins the moment the dog feels an emotional attachment to you—that is, from the moment when your rescue dog chooses you. From this point onward, the bond builds and strengthens.

You can help reinforce this bond by interacting with your shepherd. It is true that the dog will bond most with the person who spends the most quality time with her. Quality time for a shepherd means learning how to perform new obedience exercises, figuring out new hand signals, practicing agility obstacles, playing endless sessions of fetch, and any other activity that involves mental and physical stimulation.

 Fact

Dog owners tend to think that if they died, their canines would pine away and never bond with anyone else. Though a dog will certainly miss a loving owner, he will also be very willing to bond closely with a new owner. As the owner of a rescued adult, you have just as great a chance to bond with your dog as if he were a puppy.

The deeper your shepherd bonds with you, the more trusting she will become, too. When you have a dog that knows you would never put her in harm's way, you will find that you also have a more confident, outgoing shepherd.

The key to working with a rescued shepherd is to take things slowly. Allow her plenty of time to acclimate to your home and lifestyle. Most dogs settle in and begin to show their true, loving temperaments within a month of coming home. Some dogs will acclimate much more quickly; others might take a little longer.

As long as you continue to provide your adopted shepherd with good experiences and persist in your efforts to train her and keep her active, she will thrive and grow into a wonderful pet.

Nutrition

THE DAYS ARE LONG GONE WHEN it was usual to feed puppies generic puppy food and adult dogs basic, one-flavor-satisfies-all dog food. Consumers have a myriad of choices for their shepherds, but the bottom line is that you need to choose a food that meets or exceeds your German shepherd's nutritional needs. When a shepherd thrives on a food, his skin is soft and supple (no flaking), his coat is thick and full, his ribs are covered (but not buried), and his energy is boundless.

Commercial Foods

Thanks to continued research by commercial pet-food producers, the general public knows a lot more about canine nutritional needs and how to help a dog thrive rather than just survive. As you might have suspected, however, not all dog foods are quality products.

Commercial pet foods run the gamut in terms of quality. At the top end of the scale are foods made with highly nutritional, human-grade ingredients and specialized to meet a dog's particular needs. At the low end are those foods that are made with poor sources of protein, lots of filler (which adds quantity to the food but no real nutritional value), and nearly indigestible minerals and vitamins. So, how can you tell if a commercial dog food is nutritious chow or junk food?

Pet food labels can be difficult to decipher, but there are several key points to look for when trying to make sense of what's in a bag. You'll want to read the ingredients list and recognize key words that indicate the quality and quantity of the ingredients. You should also recognize the specific life stage and type of dog for which the food was developed and understand how foods are tested and trialed to meet nutrient profiles.

 **Fact**

Human-grade chicken, beef, lamb, and other meats are lower in steroids than meats approved for livestock or pet consumption. For example, chickens intended for human consumption must be fed an alternative feed a minimum of six to eight weeks before slaughter to ensure that the growth hormones and steroids are at acceptable levels in the meat.

The Association of American Feed Control Officials (AAFCO) is an association of state and federal feed officials that serves in an advisory position to state feed officials. Since each state controls its own feed regulations, the AAFCO assists in promoting standard feed regulations throughout the United States with recommended nutritional minimums (and some maximums) for dog foods. The organization also develops methods by which food companies can test their products to prove they have met the AAFCO's nutritional profiles.

Discerning Quality

For starters, when it comes to the dog food ingredient label, you should recognize that there is definitely a difference between "chicken," "chicken by-product," and "human-grade chicken." Obviously, human-grade chicken is the best. It includes meat from the chicken breasts, thighs, organs, or other parts of the chicken that are suitable for human consumption. Additionally, human-grade chicken must meet the standards set by the United States Department of Agriculture (USDA) for feeding, raising, and slaughtering the chickens.

Foods containing chicken by-product may include both digestible and indigestible parts of the chicken, anything from breast meat and organs to chicken bones, claws, feet, and feathers. The amount of indigestible chicken used in the dog food does not have to be identified, which means it is impossible for the consumer to know.

If the ingredient label lists "chicken," this indicates that chicken meat is used as the primary protein source for the food. The meat does not have to be human-grade, but it must be meat from the animal source specified (such as turkey, beef, lamb, or salmon). Lesser grades of meat will contain some organ meats, such as livers and gizzards, whereas premium grades of meat contain only meat.

Another thing to be aware of is that some pet-food manufacturers change the ingredients and the ratio of these ingredients in their foods. Depending on what is available and the market prices for various ingredients, a manufacturer may vary its pet food ingredients from batch to batch. These foods are said to be "variable formula diets."

If a food varies from batch to batch, its quality also varies, and this can affect the health of your dog. They're usually a bit more expensive, but fixed formula diets provide consistent quality. Unfortunately, the only way for the consumer to determine if a particular food is a variable or fixed formula diet is to check the ingredients labels on several bags of the food over a period of several months to determine if any changes are being made.

Life Stages

The AAFCO lists nutrition guidelines for only three life stages, two of which are lumped together. The first guideline is for puppies and pregnant or nursing females. The second is for adult dogs. While reading the packaging of a dog food, you will find wording such as, "Complete and balanced nutrition based on AAFCO guidelines for growth and reproduction" or "Complete and balanced nutrition based on AAFCO guidelines for adult maintenance."

But what about foods that claim to be developed specifically for other life stages, such as the senior dog, the active adult dog, or the less-active mature dog? Are foods developed for large-breed puppies and dogs significantly different than those designed for adult maintenance?

In general, senior foods are more digestible and richer in nutrients to compensate for the senior's decreased abilities to absorb and metabolize foods. Large-breed puppy food tends to be less rich than regular puppy food, to prevent large breeds from growing too quickly and stressing their joints. Large-breed adult dog food usually contains joint supplements to stave off arthritis and may come in larger chunks so it is not accidentally inhaled. Weight-loss foods provide good nutrition with more fill so that a dog can eat the same quantity of food, meet all nutritional needs, and lose weight.

Reputable, quality manufacturers of premium dog foods pour a lot of money into researching the specific nutritional needs of certain subsections of the canine world. The ingredients and supplements involved in a manufacturer's "designer" formulations are proprietary secrets and are not disclosed to the consumer or other manufacturers; however, they are based on available research as well as the manufacturer's own research and feeding trials.

Feeding Trials

Manufacturers can prove that their foods have met the AAFCO's recommended guidelines in one of two ways. The first is to provide a laboratory analysis of the food, showing that it contains the correct amounts of protein, fat, fiber, vitamins, and minerals. If a food has met the AAFCO's requirements in this way, the packaging will include wording like: "This food meets the AAFCO's nutrient profiles."

If a food is identified in this way, it has not undergone feeding trials. What this means to you and your shepherd is that the food may have the necessary nutrients; however, they may not be in a highly digestible form and/or the food may not be palatable. (If your dog won't eat it, he can't gain anything from it.)

What you'd like to see on the packaging is a reference to the food being "complete and balanced" and having undergone "animal feeding tests" or "animal feeding trials" using AAFCO procedures. This shows that the dogs in the trial were able to metabolize the nutrients in the food and that the dogs thrived on the food.

 Fact

Premium foods are moving away from synthetic preservatives (such as ethoxyquin) and using more natural preservatives, such as ascorbic acid (vitamin C), rosemary extract, and citric acid.

Wet, Semimoist, or Dry?

In addition to finding a food with quality ingredients and high digestibility, you'll also need to choose between wet (canned), semimoist (chewy), and dry dog foods. Canned dog foods are very tasty (to dogs). They are also easy to store, and they contain very few, if any, preservatives. As a result, however, these foods cannot be left out in a bowl for more than thirty minutes without risk of turning rancid. They are the most expensive commercial food, and because the food is soft, it doesn't help to keep a dog's teeth clean.

Semimoist foods are chewier than dry dog food. They are stored in bags, have a shorter shelf life than dry foods, and contain more sugars than other foods to keep the morsels soft. These foods often contain food coloring, too, to make them look more like human foods, like T-bone steaks, slices of cheese, and chicken drumsticks. Some dogs have difficulty metabolizing these foods and produce soft stools or more stools as a result.

▲ The right diet for your German shepherd
will provide a lifetime of good health.

Dry commercial foods promote healthy teeth and gums. They don't spoil easily, and they are the least expensive of the food types. A past complaint about dry foods was that dogs didn't find them too tasty unless they had been fed dry foods as puppies. But due to stiff competition among pet food manufacturers today, palatability seems to be a problem of the past.

Natural and Homemade

As pet owners have demanded higher-grade ingredients for their dogs, manufacturers have responded with complete lines of natural pet foods. Additionally, some pet owners feed their dogs homemade foods that may consist of all raw ingredients or a combination of raw and cooked ingredients.

For a dog food to be labeled "natural," the AAFCO guidelines require all ingredients and components of ingredients in the food to be natural and not synthetically made. If any of the vitamins or minerals is chemically synthesized, the label must state that the food is "natural with added vitamins and minerals."

Essential

If the meats in a home-prepared diet are raw, there is an increased exposure risk for both you and your dog to the bacterias E. coli and salmonella. There is some thought that freezing these meats prior to preparation may decrease this exposure risk; however, the only proven way to avoid these diseases is to cook your dog's meats thoroughly and sanitize all surfaces that come in contact with raw meats.

Home-prepared diets are those that are often recommended by holistic veterinarians. These diets include raw or cooked meats, raw vegetables, whole grains, and nutritional supplements. If prepared according to a recipe from a veterinarian with expertise in nutrition, a home-prepared diet can be an extremely healthy alternative for your shepherd.

The drawbacks to a homemade diet, however, are numerous. Personally preparing your dog's diet takes time and planning, which many dog owners can't manage. The ingredients required to make home-prepared diets are expensive and must be purchased fresh. Perhaps most importantly, home-prepared diets must be made with no substitutions, no variances in quantity, and extreme care in measuring and weighing the ingredients.

If you are considering preparing a homemade diet for your shepherd, you must consult your veterinarian. She will be able to provide you with a recipe along with help in finding sources for some of the vitamins and minerals that need to go into the mix. But whatever you do, follow this recipe to the letter; otherwise, you will be doing your shepherd far more harm than good.

Nutritional Supplementation

If a food is labeled "complete and balanced," there is theoretically no need to add supplements to your dog's diet unless they are prescribed by your veterinarian. If you are feeding a home-prepared diet, you will be adding numerous supplements to your dog's daily diet in precise measurements.

One argument for giving a dog nutritional supplements is the thought that the dog is not actually metabolizing the vitamins and minerals contained in the pet food (which is potentially true of foods that have not undergone feeding trials).

Alert!

Too much of a good thing can be harmful. Excess water-soluble vitamins, such as ascorbic acid, are flushed out of the system; however, unused fat-soluble vitamins, such as vitamins A, D, and E, can accumulate in the body organs, potentially causing serious health complications.

Another argument is that the nutritional guidelines developed by the AAFCO are minimums and that few studies have been performed to determine optimum levels of nutrients. Supplementation, therefore, is thought to be necessary to give a dog more appropriate levels. Some also argue that certain supplements serve as nutraceuticals—that is, nutrients that are prescribed at certain higher levels to treat or prevent disease. Antioxidants, such as vitamin C, might be given to boost a dog's immune system, reduce inflammation from arthritis, and/or prevent disease. Joint supplements, such as glucosamine and chondroiton sulfate, are frequently given to prevent, halt, or perhaps even reverse some of the damage from such joint diseases as arthritis and hip dysplasia.

Whether your shepherd needs nutritional supplements is a determination that should be made with the help of your veterinarian. Never attempt to supplement your shepherd's diet without knowing all the effects—both good and bad—of a particular supplement.

Feeding Puppies and Adolescents

The German shepherd is considered a large breed and has been plagued with hip abnormalities. For these reasons, many breeders are quite particular as to how they feed their pups and young dogs, being careful not to instill obesity, which would put excess strain on the dogs' joints. Breeders of large breed dogs are also concerned about foods that are so rich in nutrients that they promote danger-ously quick growth. German shepherds that grow too quickly can suffer from an assortment of bone and joint problems.

What is the correct way to feed your puppy or adolescent shep-herd? Some breeders recommend feeding a premium puppy food until the dog reaches the age of six months, at which time they suggest switching to a premium-quality active adult dog food. This allows the puppy to receive a nutrient-rich food in his early stages of development and a leaner food later to prevent overgrowth.

Another method of feeding a puppy is to use premium large-breed puppy and large-breed adult formulas, which have been devel-oped specifically to address the large-breed puppy and adult dog's needs. The pup would receive the large-breed puppy food up to one year of age and then switch over to the large-breed adult formula.

To figure out how much to feed your German shepherd puppy, use the thirty-minute method. Measure out three cups of dry dog food, and place this in the puppy's bowl. Allow your puppy to eat as much as he wants in a thirty-minute time period. Pick up the bowl after the time has elapsed, and measure how much food remains. Do this for two days to determine the correct amount.

 Fact

Puppies rarely overeat if they are given dry food. Mixing dry food with canned dog food, scraps, or broth, however, can cause a puppy to overeat—just as humans often manage to make room for dessert, even after a filling meal.

It is equally critical that you feed your shepherd enough food. One of the leading causes of aggression in puppies is hunger. With today's increasing awareness and concern about canine obesity, veterinarians are finding that puppy owners sometimes underfeed their pups. Many times, when puppy owners call the veterinarian to report behavior problems, in actuality they are describing feeding problems. Again, the proper amount to feed can be determined through the thirty-minute method.

Controlling Obesity

The most common health threat for dogs is obesity. Commercial foods taste great, so the mature dog will usually clean his plate. Some owners take this as a sign that the dog needs more food and increase the portion.

Owners enjoy being able to feed their dogs human food. This usually takes the form of table scraps, which are usually the fatty parts of meats rather than leftover vegetables. In addition to feeding calorie-laden foods as snacks, few owners take into consideration that these calories are being added to the dog's regular intake. If the dog is receiving more calories than he's burning up each day, he will gain weight.

Life-cycle changes can affect a dog's metabolism rate. The high-energy, fat-burning puppy matures, and suddenly his caloric needs drop. Additionally, spaying or neutering can lessen the shepherd's nervous energy, by eliminating his need to search for a mate, and thus cause a drop in caloric needs. If the mature shepherd continues to be fed the same portion size he received as a puppy, the shepherd is going to gain weight.

It is much easier to keep your shepherd from becoming obese than to reduce his excess weight. Keep an eye on your shepherd as he ages, and check the fat coverage over his rib cage frequently. You should be able to find each rib underneath the coat by pressing lightly with your fingers. If you have to exert more pressure to find the ribs, he's probably overweight.

Before you begin a health and fitness program for your over-weight shepherd, consult your veterinarian. She will give you exercise and feeding guidelines so that your shepherd doesn't lose too much weight too quickly.

Special Senior Needs

The only concern among seniors and geriatric shepherds (those aged eight years and older for seniors, and ten years and older for geriatrics) used to be obesity. Often, a "senior" food was actually a weight-control food. Certainly obesity can become a problem, particularly with the shepherd that is far less mobile than she has been in years past.

The more significant problem, however, tends to be as a shepherd ages, her ability to taste and digest her food thoroughly and to metabolize or extract all the necessary nutrients from her food decreases. Consequently, senior foods today are formulated to be highly palatable, very digestible, and packed with nutrients so that a senior dog doesn't have to eat more food to metabolize enough nutrients.

Healthy Snacks and Treats

A lot of the dog snacks and treats that are marketed today are made to fit a person's idea of a good snack. Copious amounts of food coloring and added salts and sugars often make these dog treats unhealthy and can cause gastrointestinal distress among more sensitive shepherds.

A better alternative is to provide wholesome snacks that are good supplements (or at least aren't detrimental) to the canine diet. Many quality pet food companies produce dog biscuits that are made with formulas similar to their premium pet foods. Also, if your shepherd enjoys fresh vegetables, he can be treated to something healthy like baby carrots without having to cut back his regular meals to compensate for any additional calories.

Essential

Because people often offer treats to each other as special rewards, it is natural for many people to reward their dogs with treats. Shepherds, however, are particularly responsive to physical interactions with their owners. In other words, a good scratch behind the ear and a pat on the back may be just as valuable to your shepherd as a treat—not to mention better for his health.

Of course, if you're looking for particularly delectable treats to use while you're training your dog, tiny bits of cheese or low-sodium hot dogs work well. An even more mouthwatering treat is tiny tidbits of baked chicken breast.

The Importance of Water

Water is necessary to flush the toxins out of your shepherd's system, to aid in digestion, and to help maintain a static body temperature—for a start. Additionally, puppies and dogs can lose a substantial amount of water through panting, exercise, and a rise in the outside temperature.

If your German shepherd has access to clean, cool fresh water at all times, he will be able to maintain his appropriate water balance on his own by drinking when he needs to. If you withhold water from your shepherd, he can quickly become dehydrated. He might also get into the habit of gorging on water if he's been without it, drinking vast quantities of water at one time because he perceives it to be a limited resource.

If you provide your shepherd with a constant supply of fresh water and he suddenly begins drinking all the time or not at all, consult your veterinarian immediately. There are several conditions that can cause a drastic change in a dog's voluntary water intake, and none of them are diseases that you want to ignore.

Grooming

THE GERMAN SHEPHERD DOES NOT HAVE extensive grooming requirements and is not considered a high-maintenance dog. If your shepherd has a double coat—hard guard hairs over a downy undercoat—he is quite literally a wash-and-go dog. Not all shepherds have a double coat, however, and at some point, regardless of your shepherd's coat type, he will need a bath—not to mention regular brushing, toenail trimming, and other routine maintenance.

Brushing

If you've purchased a puppy, your shepherd has a fuzzy puppy coat. You can anticipate this coat to shed and be replaced by her adult coat around the age of four months. Additionally, you can expect that the adult shepherd will shed in the spring and again in the fall.

During seasons when shedding is low, a weekly brushing should be all that's required to maintain a clean, smooth coat. If your shepherd likes to play in the mud, don't worry. Dried mud is easily brushed out of a double or plush coat (a double coat that has longer guard hairs giving the shepherd a very plush appearance).

Longhaired shepherds require more vigilant brushing. The setterlike coat of the longhaired dog is much more prone to matting and tangling than a plush or double coat. Twigs, burs, mud, and other small debris can create a matted mess if not attended to quickly. Occasionally, you can pick this apart with a standard comb, your fingers, or a dematting comb. Severe matting will require the attention of a professional groomer and may entail shaving off the dog's coat.

For all coats, a wire brush (a brush with metal bristles) should be used to work through your shepherd's coat. You can use a regular bristle brush; however, this brush doesn't penetrate the guard hairs very well and is more prone to miss the undercoat. Brushing once a week is fine for the adult, double-coated shepherds and most plush coats, too. Longhaired shepherds should receive daily brushing.

Puppies, regardless of coat type, should receive daily brushing. Their coats don't necessarily need it, but you want to acclimate your puppy to brushing and to being handled all over his body. He'll be a bit squirmy at first. Gently persist and reward good behavior with a small treat. Gradually increase your grooming session by thirty seconds each time until he's tolerating—and even enjoying—five minutes or more of daily brushing.

How to Handle Shedding

There is just no getting around the fact that German shepherds shed. Dog hair will appear almost everywhere in your home—in your carpets, on your clothes, and even in your soup. This is a minor nuisance when you take into account the overall joy of owning a shepherd; however, there are ways to make this problem even more manageable.

When you brush your shepherd during heavy shedding periods, brush first in the direction that the hair grows and then brush against the hair. Finish your grooming session by brushing once again in the direction of the lay of the hair, and wipe the coat with a slightly damp cloth to pick up any stray hairs and dander.

🐕 Essential

Many vacuums come with a nozzle attachment that is perfect for pet grooming. The trick is slowly acclimating your shepherd to the vacuum over a period of weeks or even months. Begin with the attachment alone, then connect it to the vacuum, and finally turn the vacuum on without touching the dog. Eventually, you will be able to use the vacuum on the dog without scaring him.

In addition to daily brushing, you may consider bathing your dog once or twice during heavy shedding periods. Washing loosens up and clears away excess hair and also removes flaking skin and trapped dirt. When your shepherd is dry, you can follow the bath with another grooming session.

Bathing

The typical adult German shepherd that is brushed on a regular basis may only need a bath three or four times a year, barring any incidents involving such activities as digging in the mud or rolling in animal dung.

If you have access to warm water outside your home and you live in a warm climate, you may choose to bathe your shepherd outdoors. Otherwise, bathing your shepherd in the bathtub usually works just fine. Here are some tips for bathing your dog indoors:

- Set out three or four clean "dog" towels for drying before you begin your shepherd's bath.
- Wash your shepherd's bedding—a clean dog on dirty bedding will undo your efforts.
- Put a nonskid surface in the bathtub, or spread out a towel.
- Use warm water.
- Shut the door to the bathroom.

- Reluctant dogs can be enticed with a treat; unruly dogs should go in rear legs first, followed by their front legs.
- A handheld showerhead helps to wet and rinse your dog.
- Don't use too much shampoo—it's hard to rinse a lot of suds out of the shepherd's undercoat.
- If you think a bath might frighten your shepherd or cause him to act aggressively, book an appointment with a professional groomer who is comfortable handling a frightened dog.
- After toweling off your dog, allow him to dry in a warm, draft-free location.
- Clean the hair out of the tub when you've finished, and change your clothes to keep from spreading wet hair around the house.

You will likely not need to frequently bathe a small shepherd puppy. However, as with brushing, it is wise to at least wet her in the tub every week so that she grows accustomed to the feel of water on her body. If you aren't diligent about this, you could end up with a seventy-pound ball of fur that *refuses* to be bathed.

Shampoos

When looking for a shampoo for your shepherd, you want to find one that has several qualities—the first being that it is formulated for dogs. Dogs have a different pH than humans, so using a human shampoo on a dog can be detrimental to your shepherd's skin. The last thing you want to do is cause an itchy, irritating, uncomfortable condition for your dog.

The shampoo should also be tearless. What this means is that if the shampoo gets in your shepherd's eyes (and it probably will), the shampoo will not cause any burning or serious discomfort. This is not to say that getting tearless shampoo in the eyes isn't uncomfortable—it is, but it's not harmful.

When faced with a full display of different dog shampoos, consider selecting one that is designed for dogs with sensitive skin. Many shepherds have skin allergies or other conditions that can be worsened by a shampoo that is too harsh. By using a shampoo that has been formulated to soothe itchy, sensitive skin, you won't accidentally exacerbate a pre-existing condition. Besides, if your shepherd's skin is healthy, using a gentle, soothing shampoo will not harm your dog in any way.

Trimming Toenails

If you regularly walk your dog on concrete surfaces for an hour or more a day, your shepherd may effectively file her nails down enough that they don't need trimming. However, most owners find that the healthy shepherd's toenails grow very quickly. To keep them from clicking as she walks on hard floors, you will probably need to trim the dog's nails every two weeks.

 **Essential**

If your shepherd is relatively tolerant of new sounds and smells, consider grinding your dog's nails with an electric nail grinder. The vibrations from the grinder, as well as the resulting sound and smell, are upsetting to some dogs. The benefits to this method are that it's fast; it leaves a smooth edge on the nail; and if you hit the quick, the heat from the grinder cauterizes the wound.

The key to clipping toenails is to keep from "quicking" the nails. Each nail has a blood supply, known as the quick, that flows nearly to the end of the nail. To keep your shepherd's nails short, you need to trim the nail almost to the quick. If you trim too far and cut into the quick, it can be painful for your dog and make quite a mess. The nail will bleed profusely, and your shepherd is likely to become frightened of the trimming process.

▲ **Proper grooming is central to your dog's hygiene.**

What makes it more difficult to trim the shepherd's nails, as compared to those of many other breeds, is that most shepherds' nails are black. You can't see where the quick ends as you can in a white or clear nail. To approximate where the quick ends in a nail, look carefully at the underside of the nail. You will see a differentiation between the nail closest to the toe and the tip of the nail. The point at which the nail becomes smooth (near the tip) consists of only nail and no quick. Clip the nail a little before the nail becomes rougher.

If you are looking at your shepherd's nails and just can't tell, clip off the very tip and then file the nail. Your shepherd will let you know when you approach the quick. If you hit the quick while filing, the dog will yelp before you are able to draw blood.

In addition to dark nails, the German shepherd is known to have a foot "thing." If you don't condition your shepherd to being handled all over, including his feet, you aren't going to be able to hold his paws to cut the nails. To prevent problems, work with your puppy daily, handling his feet and cutting the tiny nips of his nails.

Even if he has had his nails trimmed without any problems many times, an adolescent shepherd may decide to challenge you. You may have a docile, quiet shepherd one week and an ornery, snarling monster the next. Don't buy this bluff—cut those toenails anyway. Once you've gotten through a challenging toenail trimming, be prepared for a few more similar sessions. Continue to ignore your shepherd's challenges. Do not reprimand the dog verbally or physically, as this will only escalate the confrontation. However, you should reward your shepherd with a treat for each toe he allows you to trim without fussing.

Alert!

If you are totally discouraged by your shepherd's attempts to halt toenail-trimming sessions, or if you truly believe she is dangerous, contact your veterinarian immediately. Explain the situation, have the shepherd examined for any possible physical problems, and seek professional help from a veterinary behaviorist, certified animal behaviorist, or skilled trainer.

If your shepherd becomes particularly difficult to handle, go back to the basics. Trim one toenail a day. If you get good behavior on most attempts (say eight or nine in a row), increase the number of nails you trim to two per session. Then increase this to three per session, and so on. Your shepherd will eventually return to his normal behavior.

Special Cases

If you've adopted a rescue shepherd, it is very likely he has had very little experience with toenail trimming. Introducing him to this grooming task will require a lot of time and patience. In fact, before you can even begin, you'll need to work on building your shepherd's trust so he will let you touch his feet.

You can begin by showing him the clippers and rewarding him for no reaction. Next, hold the clippers near his paw without touching the nail. If the first two steps are successful, touch each of his nails gently with the clippers. Remember to reward good behavior, and ignore any fussiness.

 **Essential**

> If you are concerned that your shepherd might react to the pain of being quicked by biting or may act aggressively to dissuade you from trimming her nails, consider muzzling her while you are working. You can also arrange for a groomer to do this chore for you.

Once you've gotten your shepherd to accept the touch of the clippers to the nail, quickly clip a tiny nubbin off the end. If he doesn't respond, reward him for allowing you to do this. Take tiny clips from just a few toenails each day, being careful not to quick him. Gradually work up to trimming one paw a day, two paws a day, and then all of his toenails at once.

Eye and Ear Care

The eyes and ears are sensitive areas for most living creatures, including dogs. It is critical that both be kept free of foreign objects that could cause infection at all times. Sight and hearing problems can be difficult to detect in dogs; for this reason, all abnormal symptoms or behavior should be heeded right away.

Eye Care

Fortunately, the German shepherd breed is not plagued with eye abnormalities that require constant cleaning or with protruding eyes that require careful handling of the dog to prevent injuries. The shepherd's eyes are those of a working dog and don't require much attention.

With that said, it is possible for foreign bodies to injure your dog's eyes. Signs that indicate there might be something in her eye other than what belongs there include pawing at the eyes, rubbing eyes on the floor, squinting the eyes closed, or scratching. If you see your dog performing any of these actions, flush the affected eye with water or sterile saline solution and take your dog to the veterinarian immediately. Whether she injured her eye, has something stuck in her eye, or is suffering from the onset of disease, it is critical that the shepherd be examined as quickly as possible to prevent further damage to the eye.

Ear Care

German shepherd puppies begin with folded ears. As they grow, the cartilage in their ears grows and stiffens. For several months, shepherd puppies go through a phase in which their ears flop over—one might be up when the other isn't. Eventually, the puppy matures into an adult German shepherd with erect, open ears.

Open ears are a benefit to the dog in that there is increased air circulation in the ear canal. If a shepherd has an imbalance in the naturally occurring yeast or bacteria in the ear, the ensuing ear infection will not progress as rapidly as it would in a dog that has a flap covering the ear canal. (Ear flaps create a warm, wet area in which yeast and bacteria can multiply quickly.)

Ear infections can occur when a foreign object invades the ear canal, when impure water gets trapped in the dog's ear canal, or as a result of allergies. If you sniff your shepherd's ears on a regular basis, you will be able to tell if an infection is brewing. The smell is strong and distinct. Additionally, an infected ear will produce large amounts of foul-smelling wax, and the area immediately surrounding the ear canal will appear red and inflamed. You might also see a discharge or blood in the ear.

Alert!

If your shepherd is constantly suffering from ear infections, your veterinarian will likely refer you to an allergist. Determining the cause of a dog's allergies—such as airborne pollen or a particular food—and controlling the allergy may be the solution to your shepherd's problem.

Even if you can't see or smell the ear infection, your dog's behavior might indicate something is wrong. If she's shaking her head frequently, scratching her ears, or holding her head to one side, it is very possible that something is affecting her ears.

Do not put off seeing the veterinarian. Ear infections can move from the outer ear to the inner ear, where they are difficult to treat and can cause permanent damage. Chronic ear infections need to be treated, even if they are mild, as they can cause permanent damage to the dog's ears.

Dental Hygiene

If you want your shepherd's teeth and gums to remain healthy and pain-free throughout his life, you can't leave his dental care up to nature. Your German shepherd will need your assistance, and there are several ways that you can help. The food and treats you feed your dog, the chews and toys you give him, and the attention you pay to his dental health can make a big difference.

For starters, dry dog food is healthier for teeth and gums than wet or semimoist food because the hard kibble helps to scrape away plaque from the teeth and around the gums. Some dog foods are made specifically for dogs that suffer from gingivitis—or for dogs whose owners don't want their dogs to suffer from tooth or gum disease.

Knucklebones, hard rubber toys, and other chew items provide another opportunity for the shepherd to rid his teeth of plaque and keep his gums clean. Tied or twisted rope toys also help to remove plaque while the dog is playing.

Something else you might not know is that you can brush your dog's teeth. Your veterinarian may give you a starter kit for this. It will include a finger brush (a rubber cap with small rubber knobs on it that fits over your finger) and canine toothpaste. You can begin by rubbing the finger brush with the toothpaste over your dog's teeth and gums. As he begins to accept this, you can move up to a canine toothbrush. If you can clean your dog's teeth once a week, you'll be well on your way to preserving his dental health.

Alert!

Do not use human toothpaste to brush your shepherd's teeth! Dogs do not know how to spit and will lick off and swallow every bit of the toothpaste that's in their mouths. Human toothpastes contain fluoride, as well as whiteners, baking soda, mouthwash, and other toxic ingredients. Only use toothpastes formulated for dogs.

When you have your puppy spayed or neutered, ask your veterinarian if she can give your shepherd a fluoride treatment while he is anesthetized. If you have an older shepherd, your veterinarian may want to anesthetize him so that she can clean his teeth thoroughly before giving him a fluoride treatment. After the teeth-cleaning and fluoride treatment, your veterinarian may prescribe a wash to be squirted on your dog's teeth and gums. This solution helps to break down plaque and tartar buildup and will make your brushings a little easier.

The one thing you don't want to do is ignore your shepherd's teeth. The days of throwing the dog a bone and hoping for the best are over.

CHAPTER 11

Housetraining

THERE AREN'T MANY DOG PROBLEMS WORSE THAN frequent accidents in the house. In fact, one of the top five reasons owners give for relinquishing a dog to a shelter is that the dog is "impossible to housetrain." Unfortunately, many people simply give up when the dog does not learn right away. Housetraining does not have to be difficult. As with any other learned skill, its mastery simply requires practice and patience.

An Easy Principle

There are two key guidelines for quick and effective housetraining: Set your shepherd up for success, and eliminate virtually any opportunities for her to fail. As is true of all training, the more times your shepherd gets it right (relieves herself in an appropriate place outdoors) without getting it wrong (soiling behind the couch), the faster she will learn what it is you want her to do.

Why then is housetraining sometimes so difficult? If a German shepherd flunks Housetraining 101, it's not for lack of intelligence. She's also not taking revenge on you for not walking her last night like you promised. It's a case of pushing for too much, too soon. Most accidents happen when either a dog's boundaries (areas where she can be trusted not to soil) are expanded too quickly, or the owner asks the puppy or dog to wait too long between bathroom breaks.

Increasing Boundaries

If your shepherd has not had any accidents in her allotted space (the crate, a puppy pen, or the kitchen) for several days or a week, then you can consider increasing her space. Do not entrust her with the whole house at once. Take small steps. For example, if she's been good in her crate, move up to a crate within a puppy pen.

 **Essential**

Dog and baby gates come in different heights and widths. Gates that expand to fit a variety of widths are very useful. If you want to set a permanent boundary, such as a gate at the top of the stairs, consider installing a swinging, metal gate. It's a lot easier for family members to open and close.

What do you do if you've expanded your dog's boundaries in the house and she has an accident? First, take a look at the situation to see if you're at fault. Were you gone too long? Did you feed her and immediately put her back in the crate? If everything other than the increased boundaries has remained the same, go back to limiting her to the smaller area. When she proves reliable again, you can increase her space and try again.

Increasing Time

Your shepherd's age has a significant effect on his abilities to control his bowels and bladder. Most puppies have good bowel control by the time they are eight weeks old. However, puppies don't start having significant control of their bladders until they are at least four months old, so you really can't expect them to hold it for too long.

A young puppy will need to relieve himself roughly every two hours, as well as after eating, after playing hard, during and after walks, when he's excited, and upon awakening. But it gets better.

A four-month-old pup should be able to wait roughly four hours during the day. A five-month-old puppy could go as long as five hours without requiring a walk, and a six-month-old pup may be able to go as long as six hours, if necessary.

 Question?

> **How will I know when my dog has to go to the bathroom?**
> If a puppy or adult shepherd is in a crate and needs to relieve himself, he will whine, cry, scratch, or bark. If the shepherd is not in a crate, he may begin circling quickly, sniffing a particular spot, lifting his leg (for adults) or squatting (females and young males), or he may run behind a piece of furniture.

An adult dog, barring any physical problems or disease, *does* have complete control of his bodily functions. But you shouldn't put him in a position where he *has* to have an accident. This will make him feel ashamed and guilty. Ideally, you should never force your shepherd to wait more than four hours between potty breaks, even as an adult.

There are some dogs that are well housetrained most of the time but that get so excited they urinate when a favorite family member comes home. This is not an accident. Instead, this behavior is called submissive urination, which involves a dog showing his complete submission to another dog or person. Don't yell at the dog if this happens—it will only make matters worse. Instead, be patient. Usually, this behavior will fade as the dog matures.

The Reward System

When housetraining a puppy or adult dog, there is never any reason to use verbal or physical punishment. If you have a book that tells you to drag the dog over to an accident to punish him, throw away the book. Training a dog new skills progresses more rapidly and with better retention when a positive, reward-based training method is used.

▲ **Rewards help reinforce positive behavior.**

Using a positive, reward-based training method requires that you ignore undesired behaviors (wetting or soiling the carpet) and reward the desired behavior (relieving himself outside). Think of it this way. If one behavior is being rewarded with praise and a treat, and another behavior earns the dog nothing, which do you think the dog will choose?

When to Praise

With housetraining, knowing when to praise your dog and how to do it are important. When you take your shepherd outside, either on a leash or into a fenced backyard, wait until he is in the act of relieving himself and softly say, "Good boy." You do not want to praise him while he's sniffing or circling. This will reinforce the wrong behavior. Additionally, you do not want to use an overly excited voice to praise him while he's relieving himself—this could cause him to stop what he's doing. Keep your praises quiet, and as soon as he finishes, you can respond with more enthusiasm and give your shepherd a treat.

Alert!

Never call your shepherd and then yell at her for having an accident. Your shepherd will not relate the heated lecture with the mistake. Instead, she will think you are punishing her for coming when she was called. The next time you call her, it's very possible that she won't respond.

Believe it or not, it is possible to train your shepherd to relieve himself on command. This is particularly handy when you're in a hurry or when you and your dog are traveling. The concept is simple. When your shepherd is relieving himself, say, "Go potty" or any other command you choose. As soon as he's finished, praise and reward him. Do this every time he relieves himself. In a matter of weeks (or even sooner), your shepherd will know this command and will be motivated to relieve himself as soon as he hears it.

Crate Training

Using a crate as a tool in the housetraining process works very well. The concept of crate training is based on the fact that a puppy or adult dog does not want to soil or wet her private space. Therefore, when a dog is in a crate, she will let you know when she needs to go out. If you're not around, she will do her best to wait until you come home and walk her.

For crate training to work, however, the crate must be the correct size for the shepherd. If the crate is too big, she can soil one corner and retreat to another. This is particularly true for a puppy that is being housed in an adult's crate—there's too much space. This defeats the purpose of using a crate as a training tool.

 **Alert!**

Many people misunderstand crate training and will leave a puppy or dog in the crate virtually all the time. This is abusive to the shepherd. Your shepherd should only be in her crate if you are gone or can't supervise her—no more than a total of ten (nonconsecutive) hours per twenty-four-hour period.

Ideally, the crate should be just big enough for the shepherd to stand up without crouching, turn around without getting stuck, and lie down comfortably. If you don't want to buy a new crate every few months, you can either look into purchasing a wire crate that has dividers, or you can borrow crates from other dog owners. If you have to buy three different sizes of crates, it's still going to be a lot cheaper than replacing a precious Oriental rug or buying new wall-to-wall carpeting for your entire first floor.

Linings

You want your shepherd's crate to be comfortable, but you don't want to spend a lot of time washing wet or soiled bedding. When beginning housetraining, therefore, consider lining the crate with a thick layer of newspapers. Puppies and adult dogs may shred some of the top layer to pad their crate a little more, which is fine. With a paper lining, if there's an accident, you can simply pull out the papers and slide new papers in.

When you're more confident that your shepherd can keep his space clean, you can add some soft but easily washable towels to his thick newspaper bedding. Once he's really got the hang of things, you can buy him a nice, comfy crate pad to nestle down in.

Using a Puppy Playpen

For puppies, placing the crate in a large puppy playpen can be the perfect second step in housetraining. The pen gives a puppy more space to play in but doesn't give her too much room.

If you do use a playpen, here are a few helpful tips:

- Place the puppy playpen on a hard floor that is easy to clean.
- Put a few toys in the playpen to occupy your puppy.
- Keep your puppy's water bowl in the playpen area. This prevents spills in the crate and wet bedding.
- Use the playpen only when you are around to supervise. Shepherd puppies can climb or knock down almost anything if they are determined.
- Do not use the playpen with an adult shepherd.

Getting Creative

Another setup that could work for either a puppy or an adult shepherd includes both a crate and a dog door. You can install a dog door in a door that leads to your fenced backyard. Once this is in place, teach your shepherd how to use this door.

Show your shepherd the dog door. Push the swinging flap outward so she can see where the door leads. She'll probably want to poke her nose through and take a look. Next, go outside and leave your shepherd inside. Pull the swinging flap toward you and hold it up high so all your shepherd needs to do is walk through the opening. Reward every repetition (reversing sides to get her to come in through the door, too) with praise and a treat.

Gradually test your shepherd to see if she's getting the hang of it. Pull the flap up only slightly, and then finally, entice your shepherd to come through the door entirely on her own. To continue practicing, toss your dog's toys through the door and see if she follows after them. This learning process won't take long—even a puppy will catch on pretty quickly.

Essential

The greatest thing about a dog door is that it allows your shepherd access to the backyard at all times. However, this also means that your dog can bring the backyard in with her at all times. Muddy paws, unearthed bones, twigs, and even dead rodents are all things your shepherd can drag in through the dog door.

When your German shepherd uses the dog door without problems, you can secure your shepherd's crate to the door. This way, your puppy or adult dog has the security of your home in addition to constant access to the yard when you are out. She can relieve herself whenever she feels the need, but she won't be able to track mud all over the house if her crate is attached to the dog door.

There is one more consideration you need to make prior to installing this system in your home. Since your shepherd will likely spend most of her time in your backyard when you're away from home, it is very possible that she could annoy the neighbors with her barking. Stay on top of the situation. Give your shepherd plenty of exercise and interaction, and hopefully she will be calm and relaxed while you're away.

Food, Water, and Exercise

To improve your shepherd's rate of housetraining success, you can manipulate his feeding times and exercise schedule so that you can anticipate his need to relieve himself. When a puppy or dog drinks, the water works through his body relatively quickly—usually within an hour. When a puppy or dog eats, he will usually have a bowel movement within thirty minutes of cleaning his dish.

Planning exercise times can assist in making your shepherd's schedule more consistent, too. Exercise is very effective at stimulating bladder and bowel movements in your dog. You can expect a puppy or adult to relieve himself during or immediately after exercise and play sessions.

While a dog sleeps, his body produces a hormone that slows the production of urine. However, if he takes a long drink right before he retires for the night, he will need to relieve himself again. One way to help young puppies and learning adults make it through the night is to remove the water bowl one hour prior to bedtime. Then, right before he retires to his crate, send him out one more time to relieve himself.

 **Fact**

Spaying of large-breed female dogs can cause incontinence—from very mild to severe. Fortunately, the female can be supplemented with the hormone that she's no longer producing in adequate supply, and this usually solves the situation.

Of course, removing the dog's water only works if your shepherd is calm and relaxed and nearly ready for sleep. If, on the other hand, he is out with the kids playing an endless game of fetch, he will need his water. Try to limit his evening activities during that last hour before bedtime, if you can. If you can't, allow him to drink water, but be prepared to wake up later in the night to let him out.

Schedules

Single people work. Married people often both work. In some cases, a spouse may stay at home or work from home, but rarely does a dog owner have the perfect arrangement for housetraining a puppy or an adult dog. If you're flexible, creative, and willing to work around your shepherd's needs, you can find a way to spend time with your dog without disrupting your work schedule.

Puppies require the most work. In general, they need to be let out every three hours and fed three times a day. The untrained adult dog can hold out longer; however, he, too, needs a midday break because he is confined to a crate during the day. If your trained adult dog has a dog door, he can go in and out at will. Otherwise, he will require a midday break as well.

Alert!

If you own an adult shepherd that is accident-free for weeks, months, or years but suddenly has a random accident, or several accidents, take him to the veterinarian immediately. Don't assume it's incontinence or old age. It could be a urinary tract infection, pain or numbness in the spine, a tumor, or infected anal sacs, to name just a few possibilities.

If you work outside the home, you're probably a bit worried—you can't take off of work whenever your shepherd needs you. If this is your scenario, you'll need to consider several options.

One possibility is doggie day care. Your dog will have a blast, as long as the day care is run well—check references thoroughly. These facilities can cost as much as a week of child care and could be as much as $1,000 per month. Option two is to hire a pet walker or pet sitter to come into your home as often as necessary. Going rates for these services vary but could cost between $8 and $15 per visit. Another option is to ask for the help of a trusted neighbor, friend, or relative. Note that you must trust this person to come every day and do all the right things with your dog.

You can make almost any situation work with patience and persistence. Just remember that your shepherd needs consistent, reliable scheduling and care to trust you and feel secure. As long as you have the dog's best interests at heart, a plausible solution will present itself.

Simple Cleanup

German shepherds are fast learners, and they aim to please. Housetraining usually goes very quickly, but your dog is bound to make mistakes along the way. To protect your floors and carpets, you need to be prepared for the worst. This means having several different cleaning products, as well as rags and paper towels on hand at all times.

 **Fact**

Many owners restrict their shepherds to hard surfaces in the home that are easy to clean, such as sealed tile floors or laminate, vinyl, or urethane flooring. Urine or feces will not penetrate these surfaces, and it is possible to get completely rid of the odor.

When you find stool on a carpet, first remove as much of the solid matter as possible. Blot up any liquids with an absorbent paper towel. Then use a pet cleaner specifically designed for carpeting, following the directions carefully. For urine, blot up as much as possible from the carpet with paper towels, continuing until you can get no more liquid to appear on the towels. Then clean with a pet cleaner made to break down the chemical components of urine so that the spot no longer smells. Again, follow the directions on the package.

With both kinds of accidents, the sooner you can clean it up, the better chance you have of neutralizing the smell and removing any stain. If accidents happen during training, do not punish the dog. As mentioned before, punishing bad behavior is not nearly as effective as ignoring it and rewarding good behavior. Just do your best to clean up accidents, and continue training your dog with patience and understanding.

CHAPTER 12

Socialization

POSSIBLY THE MOST CRITICAL NEED your German shepherd has is to be socialized. A socialized dog is one that is comfortable around all kinds of people and dogs, in any location and under any circumstances. The German shepherd is not a naturally social breed. Left to her own devices, she will become increasingly protective and territorial and could perceive every passing person or dog as a threat. Socialization is an absolute necessity.

Why Do It?

The German shepherd is bred to be wary of strangers and highly perceptive of her environment. She is protective of those she loves and territorial when it comes to her home, yard, and vehicles. She would give her life—without hesitation—to protect her caring and trustworthy owner.

But, the German shepherd isn't perfect—no dog is. They make mistakes. They misjudge situations, particularly if they haven't had similar past experiences. The only way your shepherd can make the right decisions is if she learns to differentiate between threatening and nonthreatening situations.

Your dog must learn that the crying baby, the wobbly toddler, and the two young children who are constantly cutting across the front yard are not dangerous. She needs to realize that she can bark to alert you when the deliveryman brings packages to the door, but she can't burst outside and bite him. She needs to be able to discern that the elderly woman with a cane and the teenager swinging his book bag while walking to the bus stop are not threatening or carrying deadly weapons.

Question?

If I socialize my shepherd, will he still protect me?
Absolutely. Socialization does not make your shepherd a wimp. In fact, it is just the opposite. Only the well-socialized dog is mentally strong enough to distinguish between truly threatening and non-threatening situations and to protect your family when you are really in danger.

To accomplish the goal of owning a trustworthy, socialized shepherd, you will have to do some work. You'll have to continue working on socialization throughout the life of your shepherd to maintain your dog's good attitude toward people. It's a big responsibility, but a diligent owner will be rewarded tenfold.

Socializing with People

The key to socializing a puppy or a rescued shepherd is to make sure that while you are introducing your shepherd to new people and acclimating him to a variety of different settings, you are keeping the sessions positive. All it takes is one distressing experience to set back your shepherd in his training.

Since the situations you put your dog in are out of his control, you have to be his ambassador. It is up to you to make sure your puppy or adult dog is comfortable at all times. If someone is doing something that you know is going to frighten your shepherd, you *must* step in to prevent a bad experience.

🐕 Alert!

Some behaviorists believe that the way a puppy is raised and the experiences he has may make up to 60 percent of his final character, giving "nurture" more clout than "nature." Unless you socialize your puppy, he won't develop his best possible temperament.

Puppies

A puppy is born with a predisposition for a certain temperament, which will develop at maturity. Environment, however, plays a key role in determining whether the puppy reaches her full potential as a social dog. In other words, a puppy that is predisposed to be timid and fearful can overcome her fears if she is raised in the right environment. Likewise, a puppy predisposed to be a terrific, friendly dog could be permanently stunted in a harsh and isolated environment.

There's also a sense of urgency in socializing a puppy. Your puppy is most impressionable in terms of learning social skills before she reaches twelve weeks of age. If you used a reputable breeder, he likely gave your puppy an excellent start by having friends, neighborhood children, and others come over to handle and play with the puppies. If your breeder wasn't conscientious and kept the puppies in a dark barn, the pressing need to socialize your puppy is greatly increased.

If you have a puppy, start socialization work immediately. Some experts feel that the puppy should meet 100 strangers within the first twelve weeks of life and visit fifty new places. That's a lot of stimulation. A good start would be to set a goal of meeting at least one new person every day and visiting two or three new locations each week.

When you visit new locations, encourage your puppy to check everything out. Give her treats to reward good, friendly behavior. Encourage people to pet her so she learns to enjoy handling by different people. Give treats to strangers to offer her so that she associates an outstretched hand with something good.

Your puppy should be comfortable with everyone in your family—extended relatives included—and anyone who regularly works in your home. For example, if you have children, make sure the babysitter and the puppy are on excellent terms. You don't want to come home to find your sitter trapped in the bathroom with the shepherd standing guard outside the door. She probably won't work for you again.

Rescued Dogs

The rescue dog comes with the experiences of her early life. For many shepherds that wind up in shelters, this past is overwhelming. Fortunately, this likely won't be a problem you need to worry about. If you've rescued a German shepherd from a good shelter or a breed rescue, you will know your shepherd's temperament, weaknesses, and strengths. Your job is to improve upon a solid start.

 **Fact**

Trust in humans is perhaps the biggest hurdle for a rescue that has been hurt or neglected by her previous owner. The fact that this shepherd trusted you enough to pick you speaks volumes about your potential influence on her. However, it could be months before she gives you her total trust.

Start your shepherd off slowly. Working with what already makes her comfortable is a confidence builder. In other words, if you adopted a shepherd that adores children, start introducing her to as many children in as many places as possible. Reward her with treats for good behavior. As she becomes more and more self-confident, begin introducing her to adults.

When introducing your shepherd to strangers, watch her body language carefully. If you see any signs that she's getting anxious, stressed, or frightened, you've pushed her out of her comfort zone. Take her out of the situation immediately. Dogs bite out of fear more than for any other reason.

Fearful Puppies and Adults

A fearful puppy or adult dog is twice the responsibility of a stable, friendly shepherd, and it requires dedication, time, and patience to draw him out of his shell. But bashful pups need love too, and enough time and care from you can turn yours into a delightful dog. Whatever you do, don't use your shepherd's shyness as an excuse not to introduce him to people or to take him places.

Whether working with a puppy or adult shepherd that is timid, you need to be acutely aware of the subtle body language he will exhibit as he becomes increasingly stressed. When a dog is frightened, his ears may rotate back a little. He might begin panting, crouch slightly, tuck his tail in between his legs, or shake. He might also back up or start leaning into you.

Whatever you do, don't force your shepherd to meet anyone. This is not only terrifying to your shepherd, it could also be dangerous for the stranger. The other thing you don't want to do is coddle a frightened shepherd. If you try to comfort your scared shepherd by stroking him and saying, "It's okay, sweetie," he will think you are rewarding him for his fearful behavior. Instead, move him far enough away from the person so that he is no longer worried. Let him observe the stranger from what he considers a safe distance. Reward him with praise and rubs only when he is no longer anxious or showing any signs of stress.

Shy shepherds are highly sensitive to strangers' body language, movements, and overall demeanor. For this reason, it is important to know the actions that may upset a timid dog. Some of the things a dog might find threatening include:

- Direct eye contact
- Hand outstretched above the dog's head
- Squatting down to the dog's level
- Face in the dog's face
- Sharp, loud voice
- Leaning over the dog's back

If you are making introductions for your dog, tell people not to look him in the eye or pet him, and tell them to let the dog approach them. This will help your shepherd feel much more comfortable with the strangers he meets.

Essential

If your shepherd is finding it hard to meet other people on his own, consider asking a friend who owns a very sociable dog (and one that your shepherd enjoys being with) to come with you and your dog. The bolder dog can give your shepherd the support he needs to get over his fear of certain kinds of people.

Fearful shepherds require a lot of work to help them overcome their fears. This is not to say that your efforts won't be rewarding. Watching a shepherd's confidence grow (however slowly) all because of your tireless efforts is an amazing feeling. Some shepherds may never be totally comfortable with all people and all situations. Your help, however, will make a significant improvement.

Adjusting to Everyday Things

For puppies, everything is new. Normally, the first time a puppy sees or hears something unusual in your home, it will startle her. The second time she is exposed to the same thing, she will be curious. By the time she experiences the stimulus a third time, the puppy will have figured out that it is nothing to be afraid of and will ignore it. During this process, don't react to the puppy's startled or curious behavior. She will become more comfortable in time.

Adult rescue dogs tend to find more things in the home startling than puppies, largely because these dogs often haven't had much experience living in a house with a family. The flush of the toilet, the hum of the vacuum, or the slam of the door could really startle your dog. For this reason, you need to be prepared to act appropriately when your dog gets caught off guard.

Basically, this is the same method that you would use with a puppy. If your shepherd is terrified when you turn on the garbage disposal, don't respond to her reaction. Your dog's reaction is not punishable behavior—it's natural. Simply ignore her fearful responses and reward her when she doesn't respond at all.

 **Alert!**

If your shepherd is afraid of something outside, such as a school bus, do not drag her closer to it. Move away from the bus until she is at a comfortable distance. Let her watch. Then reward her with praise and a treat. Every day, bring her a little closer to the bus, rewarding her for calm or curious behavior and ignoring any fearful responses.

Another method of helping your shepherd if she is afraid of something is through desensitization. Using this method, you increase your dog's exposure to the stimuli that frighten her. With thunderstorms, for example, you would play tapes of thunderstorms in the home. In theory, she will learn over time that nothing happens to her during a thunderstorm, and her fear during an actual storm will decrease. With this method, you would also ignore any signs of fear that she might show and reward calm behavior.

Introducing Friendly Dogs

In addition to socializing your shepherd with all kinds of people, you'll need to socialize him with other dogs, too. This may not seem as critical; however, if you've ever attempted to walk a shepherd that is lunging and barking at every dog he sees, you can appreciate the importance of owning a dog-friendly shepherd. Your neighbors will appreciate it, too.

If you own a puppy, begin by introducing him to well-trained dogs that you know are friendly and fully vaccinated. You can introduce the puppy and dogs in a neutral area (a place that neither puppy nor dog will claim as his own), allowing the puppy to approach the adult dog. Even though you've chosen very friendly dogs for your puppy to meet, watch the adult dog carefully for any signs of aggression or attempts to control the puppy.

 Fact

Dogs that are loose when introduced tend to have fewer confrontations than those that are leashed. It is thought that the leash makes a dog feel he has less ability to escape or more responsibility to protect you. Before you let your puppy play loose (in a fenced area) with a friendly, vaccinated dog, make sure that the dog's owner can reliably recall her dog.

You and your pup should attend puppy classes as soon as your shepherd is fully vaccinated (usually around fourteen to sixteen weeks). These classes typically include a puppy socialization period prior to the training portion of the class in which the puppies are allowed to romp and play together. The play can sound pretty rough, but for the most part, this is no reason to panic. Playing with other puppies of the same age is one of the ways your puppy will learn good bite inhibition. If he bites a puppy too hard, the puppy won't play with him, which is truly a punishment he will learn from.

If you see that your puppy is bullying or picking on another puppy that is becoming distressed, quietly walk up to your puppy and hold his collar. If he's still attacking the other puppy, firmly say, "No!" and calmly remove your puppy from the play group. Have him sit next to you for a minute, praise him for his good behavior, and then allow him to continue playing.

If your puppy is on the receiving end of a bully's attention, allow him the opportunity to communicate to the bully that he is upset. If he tries and fails or if he is obviously becoming distressed, step in. Remove your puppy from the situation and consult with the overseeing trainer. The bully should be removed from play.

Adult Dog Socialization

If you've adopted an adult shepherd, the shelter or rescue should be able to tell you whether or not your shepherd is dog friendly. If your shepherd is aggressive toward dogs, don't throw in the towel. Behaviorists feel that dog/dog aggression (or fear aggression) is one behavior that can be modified. (For more information on working with a dog aggressive shepherd, see Chapter 14.)

▲ Socialization is necessary for all German shepherds.

If your adopted shepherd is thought to be good with other dogs, that's great. Give her lots of opportunities to meet other (friendly) dogs of all shapes and sizes. Dog parks can be great places for your shepherd to play and meet other dogs; however, they can make for bad experiences if things get out of hand.

Alert!

On occasion, you will find an owner of a small or toy breed who does not want your shepherd loose in the park. Though you know your shepherd is gentle, and your shepherd has every right to play in the park, it is better to be polite and wait until the little dog leaves.

A dog park is only as good as the people who are there with their dogs. Aggressive, controlling dogs aren't supposed to be allowed in dog parks; however, there's always someone who enjoys breaking the rules. Before you allow your shepherd to play with others at a park, watch the dogs carefully for antagonistic behavior. Talk to the owners, too, to find out more about their dogs.

Other Canine Pets

If you already own an adult dog and are bringing home a puppy, there are several things you can do to help ease any tension between them. The best pairings are usually between dogs of opposite sexes. If you own a male dog, bringing home a female puppy is likely to be more successful than bringing home another male. You should also be sure to spay or neuter your adult dog. This will help calm the dog and ease any sexual tension.

You might also consider keeping your adult dog at a boarding kennel or a friend's house for several hours when you first bring the puppy home. This will allow the puppy to become familiar with his new surroundings on his own. This will also establish the puppy as part of the household before the adult dog comes home. (This is the same technique that is sometimes used with children when parents bring a new baby into the home.) The adult dog finds the presence and scent of the puppy far less confrontational if he is already there than if he is suddenly introduced into the home.

It's also important to supervise the two dogs' activities together. Separate the puppy and the adult dog when you can't supervise, and don't allow the older dog to harass the puppy or play too roughly. If the adult dog does become obnoxious with the puppy, hold his collar. Tell him, "No!" and walk him over to his crate for a two-minute timeout. He should quickly learn that beating up the puppy won't get him anywhere. If his aggressiveness toward the puppy escalates, seek professional help immediately.

A final important point to remember is to always provide your adult dog with an escape from the puppy. He should have his own crate filled with his own special toys to which the puppy does not have access. You might find that your adult dog puts up with the puppy pretty well. Just keep in mind that your shepherd puppy can be extremely active, and this can drive even the most agreeable dogs a little crazy.

 **Fact**

As in wolf behavior, two male dogs that can't seem to get along will typically fight until they've decided who is alpha, or dominant. Two female wolves (or dogs) vying for the alpha position will often fight until one is killed.

A Second Adult

Bringing a second adult dog into the home can be a bit trickier than bringing home a puppy. If one of the two adult dogs is submissive, things are usually okay. It also helps if the adult dogs are of the opposite sex and altered. However, if both dogs want control and are of the same sex, you might have a major problem on your hands.

Allowing the new dog to acclimate for a few hours or days while the older dog is boarded or at another home may help the older dog accept the new dog. Introducing the two dogs on neutral territory is a good idea. After they've made friends and are playing together, you can bring the two dogs home.

For the first few months, always keep an eye on the dogs when they are together, and separate them when you can't watch. If the older dog is dominant, it could take the new, adopted dog up to a month before she feels comfortable enough in her surroundings to stand up for herself. Once she does, the older dog may back off and the two could settle comfortably in their roles. But if the dogs still haven't found a way to get along after a few months, it may just be an unsuccessful match.

Where to Get Help

Socializing puppies and adults with people and other dogs can be a breeze with many shepherds. It can also be frustrating with shepherds that are exceptionally fearful or extremely dominant or controlling. If you own a puppy or rescued adult that falls into either extreme category, it is critical that you give your shepherd the help he needs to overcome his problems.

Before you choose someone to work with, make sure you are comfortable with the individual's training techniques and methods. Many trainers still believe that the only way to handle an aggressive dog—that is, a dog exhibiting fear-based or control-based aggression—is to manhandle the dog. This is especially true when trainers are dealing with a large guarding-type breed, such as the shepherd. However, this type of handling will only exacerbate the problem.

First, call the breeder or breed rescue from whom you purchased or adopted your shepherd. Explain exactly what kinds of problems you are having and how you've been attempting to handle the situations. If this person can't help you, he will refer you to someone who can. There might be a good trainer or veterinarian behaviorist in the area who works with fearful or dominant dogs. You might also be referred to a certified animal behaviorist or a veterinary technician who has a special interest in animal behavior.

Alert!

Working with a difficult shepherd is not a project for a novice dog owner or a first-time shepherd owner to tackle alone. Don't be embarrassed or reluctant to seek help. The sooner you get this problem taken care of, the easier your life will be.

Take the time to find a trainer who is successful, has excellent references, and uses positive, reward-based training. Make sure she is comfortable working with German shepherds and that you are comfortable with her training style. After all, *she* will be training *you* to train your shepherd.

CHAPTER 13

Puppy Parenting

THERE'S A REASON WHY PUPPIES are so cute. If they weren't, few owners would put up with the things they do. Actually, that's part of the problem. If you allow your shepherd puppy to do "cute" things when she's little, you may be stuck with those no-longer-so-cute antics later, when she weighs sixty pounds (and still thinks she's a puppy).

One strategy is to apply the rules you set for your children to your puppy as well. Ask yourself this: Would you allow your daughter to hit you if she didn't want her fingernails trimmed? Would you let your son push you out of the way to charge through the door? How about letting your nephews jump out of the car and run into traffic? The answer, of course, is no. So why would you let your shepherd puppy get away with this kind of behavior?

Needle Teeth

Puppies are very oral. They don't have hands, so they can't pick things up and examine them the way a small child would. Instead, puppies use their mouths to taste, feel, and carry things. Because of the way puppies explore their worlds, a common issue for the shepherd puppy owner is that her puppy is biting. Even if the bites aren't too hard, those little needle teeth can really hurt!

When your puppy was with his mother and littermates, if he bit another puppy too hard, that littermate would scream and refuse to play with him. If your puppy chomped down too hard on his mom, he got a swift but controlled correction that likely made him shriek—not out of pain but as a terrified apology). Your puppy and his littermates were all learning "bite inhibition," or the ability to control biting, whether in play or as a defensive reaction.

Now your puppy no longer has his mother and littermates to help him continue learning, and it will be at least six to eight weeks before you can enroll him in a puppy class where he can continue to learn this necessary skill. In the meantime, you are in charge of this vital training.

You have to let your puppy know that hard bites are unacceptable but that controlled mouthing is okay. When your puppy bites too hard, yelp loudly, turn your back on him, and ignore him. If he's not going to play nicely, you're not going to play at all. After several minutes, you can go back to playing with your pup, praising him calmly if he's mouthing gently. It shouldn't be long before your puppy catches on that hard biting is not allowed.

 **Essential**

Does your puppy tend to nip the most when you first walk in the front door? When you leave, place a chew toy by the front door that you can carry in with you. Before your puppy has a chance to greet you at the door with teeth, give him the toy. He can't nip you if he's got something in his mouth.

Another form of biting that a shepherd might exhibit, particularly if he's from lines with strong herding instincts, is nipping at or gripping people's heels. Running children are prime targets for this kind of behavior; however, some dogs will nip adults, too. Here are a few tips to help make this herding instinct more manageable:

- Don't permit people to run inside the house.
- Yelp if you are nipped and ignore the puppy.
- Praise your puppy when he follows you without nipping at your heels.
- Don't let anyone laugh when the puppy nips. He will take this as a reward for his behavior.

Barking

The German shepherd is not a particularly "barky" breed. When a shepherd barks, it is usually for a reason: a stranger at the door, a dog in the front yard, or someone lurking behind the fence. If a puppy is bored, left outside unattended for hours on end, or inadvertently encouraged to bark incessantly when someone is at the front door, an annoying problem could develop.

The first solution to a puppy's excessive barking is to increase his exercise and play times, including more outings and social interactions and participation in obedience training or another performance sport. If the barking was a result of boredom or lack of exercise, these actions should solve the problem.

If you're leaving your pup outside unattended during the day or for hours during the evening, bring him in! He's barking because he's not getting the attention from you that he needs. German shepherds are not outdoor dogs that can amuse themselves for hours on end. They were bred to work with their owners. If you can't give your puppy the time and attention he needs, he's going to find destructive ways to entertain himself. Barking is one of the habits that might arise in a neglected shepherd.

Another way to decrease random bouts of barking is to train the dog to bark on command. As ironic as this sounds, teaching a puppy to perform a behavior on command lessens his desire to do it if he's not going to be rewarded. If there's no longer any benefit to his random barking, he will probably stop doing it altogether.

Another advantage to teaching your puppy to bark on command (and to hush on command, too) is that when he's fully grown and has a deep bark, you can have him bark if you need to frighten away a thief, a wild animal, or any other unwanted guest. Whomever you want to frighten off will have no idea that your shepherd is barking on command—nor will he want to linger to find out why your shepherd is barking.

Alert!

For a dog, sometimes even negative attention (such as shouting, stern looks, etc.) is seen as a reward for the behavior. One of the best ways to extinguish an undesirable behavior is to ignore it, rewarding the shepherd with attention and treats only when he isn't barking.

To teach a dog to bark on command, wait until your shepherd is barking and say, "Speak!" You can use a hand signal, too, if you want to be able to signal your shepherd to bark without a verbal command. Praise and reward him for barking. When he stops barking, give the command "Hush!" or "Enough!" and praise him, rewarding him with a treat. Continue working on these commands every day, being careful never to yell at him to stop barking. You will notice that over a period of weeks or even days your puppy will have reduced his random barking substantially.

Continue to work on the commands—anticipate when he is just about to bark, and then give him the bark command. He will soon be able to respond when he isn't barking or preparing to bark. If he doesn't respond to the command, go back to giving the commands while he is performing the correct behavior.

Digging

Like barking, digging is not a shepherd-specific trait. However, it is a behavior common among bored puppies. Again, the solution to this problem is more exercise, more interaction, more training, and less time alone—particularly outside where your pup or dog can dig.

There are some shepherds that will smell rodents underground and dig to get to them. Other puppies enjoy unearthing bulbs—many of which are poisonous when eaten—and shrubs. Some shepherds like to bury bones and then unearth them later. Older male puppies, those that have reached physical maturity, may dig under the fence in an attempt to reach a female in season; neutering solves this digging problem. In general, if you don't want your shepherd digging in the backyard, supervise her while she's outside. When she begins to dig, distract her with another activity for which you can praise her.

▲ **Keeping your dog occupied with activities
will help eradicate unwanted behaviors.**

If the location in which your puppy is digging is more of a problem than the fact that she is digging, block your puppy from that part of the yard. If you have a pup that enjoys burying her bones, you can select an area specifically for burying and digging up bones. To teach her that this is her digging space, choose a plot of about four by four feet, and bury a couple of bones in the ground. When the puppy digs and buries bones in the digging plot, praise her.

The digging plot requires that you supervise most of your puppy's activities in the yard to make sure she is praised for using the correct area of the yard. Over time, if your puppy has a treasure to bury, she will automatically go to her digging plot.

Chewing

Chewing is a natural way for a puppy to clean his teeth. Many dogs find chewing to be a calming activity, too. As your puppy begins to lose his milk teeth to make room for his adult set, chewing becomes a method of pain relief for itchy, raw, and throbbing gums.

Essential

Puppies start losing their milk teeth around four to five months of age. The teething period only lasts a month or so from beginning to end, but it may seem like a whole lot longer to a puppy in pain—and to the owner who finds that her table legs have been chewed.

As a general rule, your shepherd puppy should have access to lots of quality, safe chew toys and bones. This is particularly crucial during his teething period. Of course, a full supply of appropriate chew items doesn't mean that your puppy will walk right by your leather shoes without nibbling. The loss of a favorite shoe can be aggravating, but remember that your puppy can't chew your shoes—or anything else—if he doesn't have access to them.

To avoid chewing damage, do two things. First, limit your puppy's access to forbidden items. Close the doors to bedrooms and closets, and keep all personal items off the floor. Clear coffee tables of all trinkets. If you have children, keep action figures and toys stowed away.

Second, supervise your puppy's activities in the home. If he's not in the room with you, you won't know what he's up to. Use baby gates to keep him near you, or consider tying a long leash from his collar to your belt. If he does grab something he shouldn't, don't chase him; this makes it a game. Instead, hold a treat so he knows you have something for him, and offer the goodie in exchange for the item he's holding. Praise him for swapping the item for the treat, and put the item out of reach and out of sight.

Jumping Up

A big problem among all breeds of dogs is jumping. Most dogs have the impulse to jump up on a person if they're excited to see him. It's a way of showing deference. If you watch a litter of puppies, you will see that they all hop up to lick their mother's face. However, jumping can become quite a nuisance, especially if there are muddy paws involved.

 Fact

When you see two dogs together, you might see one dog reaching up to lick the other dog's muzzle and lips. The dog that is licking is the more submissive of the two dogs and is showing the other dog respect. You will not see the dominant dog return the compliment.

You don't want your shepherd jumping up on your frail great aunt when she comes over to visit, nor do you want your puppy bowling over the neighbor's kids. But you don't want to suppress your puppy's good intentions either. You have many options to control the situation. You can get down on the dog's level; teach "Jump up" as a command; substitute an alternate behavior that the shepherd finds rewarding; or ignore the behavior to extinguish it completely.

Get Down on His Level

As soon as you walk in the door, kneel or squat down to your puppy's level. From this vantage point, give him the rubbing and attention he wants and allow him to slather you with puppy kisses. As your puppy grows and matures, he will recognize that you are going to allow him to greet you on his level. His reason for jumping up on you, children, and others will no longer exist.

Teach "Hugs" on Command

When you come in the door and you know your puppy will jump up on you, kneel down and pat your shoulders or chest, saying, "Hugs." (You can substitute any command you'd like.) Praise your puppy when he jumps up on your shoulders and gives licks. Do not praise him if he jumps up on you when you haven't given him the "Hugs" command. Soon, he will recognize that he gets the attention he wants and is allowed to show you deference only when you give him the command or signal to do so.

Substitute an Alternate Behavior

Another approach is to give your shepherd something to do instead of jumping up. For example, if friends are coming over, instruct them to ignore the puppy unless he sits, in which case they can pet him. You can put him in a sit five feet back from the front door and require him to stay while your friends enter. (It's okay to help a young puppy to maintain his stay by keeping your hands on him.) After your friends have entered, they can reward him with rubs, treats, and verbal praise.

Ignoring the Puppy

A very effective way to extinguish a behavior is to ignore it. In this instance, you would walk in the front door, put away your things, and sit and read for five minutes without making any contact with your puppy. He should settle down relatively quickly. Once he's relaxed, you can gently rub him and praise him for his calm demeanor.

🐶 Alert!

If you are ignoring a behavior to extinguish it, you must be consistent. The most common mistake an owner makes is to slip up and shout at the shepherd. Though this seems like a negative response, it could be perceived as a reward by the dog. If you do anything other than ignore the behavior, you're sending a mixed message, and the jumping will continue.

When working to extinguish a behavior, be aware that the behavior will get worse before it gets better. Just be patient with your dog, and hang in there. The reward for your efforts will come soon.

Separation Anxiety

A common problem among German shepherds is separation anxiety. This means that a dog becomes panicked whenever his owner leaves him at home. This occurs with both puppies and adults. A puppy may react more strongly, having already endured the separation from his mother and littermates.

With separation anxiety, the situation often seems much more serious than it really is. Remember, the shepherd is one of the most intelligent canine breeds. If your puppy cries out from his crate as you open the door to leave the house, your turning back to give him one last pet will reward his behavior. This teaches him that his cries will win him more attention from you.

You can help the worried puppy deal with your departure by giving him a particularly delicious chew toy or bone. Many dogs find chewing to be a comforting behavior. If your puppy has an interesting and tasty treat in his crate when you leave, he won't dwell on the fact that you're gone.

Desensitization training works for separation anxiety, too. The key to using this training method is to figure out your routine prior to leaving the house. Putting on your jacket, picking up a set of keys, tying your shoes, turning off the lights, and opening the door could all be clues that your puppy associates with your leaving him alone.

 **Essential**

> If you suspect that your puppy continues howling, crying, and barking the entire time you are gone, set up a tape recorder to record his behavior. You'll likely find that as soon as you leave the house, the puppy quiets down and goes to sleep. The dramatic crying and whining is just his effort to keep you there.

To desensitize him to these sounds and actions, perform these behaviors frequently throughout the day *without leaving*. Then intermittently leave the house but come right back inside. If your puppy is behaving better, leave the house for a longer period of time, continuing to provide all the clues that indicate you are leaving. Soon, these clues will no longer signify that you are leaving, and your shepherd will have less opportunity to work himself up. Additionally, you are teaching your puppy that you always come back.

Though most canine separation anxiety is relatively mild and treatable, some dogs do exhibit alarming behavior when left alone. If you notice that your shepherd is causing destruction to his crate, your home, or himself, seek professional help immediately.

Bolting

After a young puppy has been in a crate too long and has had an accident, the last thing you want is the very first thing she will do: bolt from the crate as soon as the door is opened. Pushing, shoving, or bolting behavior is also commonly seen when the door to the house or a car door is opened. The first situation is mostly an inconvenience; the latter two situations are dangerous. A loose shepherd that has bolted due to excitement will often not look where she is going—she could be hit by a passing car or get lost. This is especially true of puppies and untrained adults that do not yet have reliable recall skills.

Fortunately, with a little training, you can have a shepherd that will not try to run out the front door, car door, or crate door as soon as she spots an opportunity. Instead, she will remain in a sit-stay until you give her the okay signal.

"Wait" Training

The procedure for training the "Wait" command is relatively simple. First, put a leash on your puppy. Then have her sit and stay (that is, put her in a sit-stay) by the front door. As soon as she's sitting, give the command "Wait." Open the door a few inches and then shut it. If she breaks her sit-stay, place her back in position. Open and shut the door again. If she retains her position, give your release command, "Okay!" and praise her. Continue working on this step until she doesn't even lurch forward in anticipation when the door opens.

Next, put her in a sit-stay and again give the command "Wait." Open the door and take a step toward it as if you're headed out. Then step back, shut the door, give your release command, and praise your obedient shepherd.

Essential

When boarding your dog at a kennel facility or leaving her with a friend or relative, tell the person that your shepherd is trained to wait. Give him the release command so he can use it when taking your dog out of her kennel. A well-trained shepherd may very well refuse to budge until she's given the release command.

Continue adding steps until you can walk out the door and back in, and then finally step out the door and stand for thirty seconds or more with your shepherd in a sit-stay inside. The same strategy can be used with the car door. Keep the dog on a leash, tell her "Wait," and open the car door. Start out by waiting for just a second and then releasing her. Next, wait several seconds before you release. Continue working with her until you can swing the door wide open and step away from the car while she remains seated in the car. Your release command should be the only thing that gives her permission to move.

Growing Up Is Hard to Do

FOR MANY DOG BREEDS, THE HARDEST PART—raising the puppy—is over by the time the dog is twelve months old. For the German shepherd puppy owner, however, the difficulties are just beginning at this age. During adolescence, the shepherd has almost reached his full height. He is sexually mature and beginning to fill out. This is also the time period during which a shepherd will challenge his owner, test the boundaries of his home, and need more exercise than ever.

Just Like Teenagers

Canine adolescence is very similar to the human teenage years. Just like human teens, adolescent dogs have a very strong desire to challenge authority. Though he can't speak to you, your dog will still find ways to talk back to you. He'll also overstep many of the boundaries that he respected as a puppy. This time can be very frustrating, but just as with human teens, adolescence is an awkward phase that always passes eventually.

By the time your shepherd hits adolescence (between ten and twenty-four months of age), he will start looking for and noticing certain opportunities. If the rules pertaining to home and family have been lax and inconsistent, your dog is going to push his limits. He will try to gain as much control as possible until someone puts him in his place.

This does not mean that one day, out of the blue, your shepherd is going to turn on you and become a destructive menace. Challenges to owners are far more subtle, which is often the root of the problem. The challenges begin so imperceptibly that many owners don't realize they're being challenged until they suddenly won't put up with a behavior any more—and the shepherd responds with a growl, snarl, or snap.

 **Fact**

It is true that some shepherds never challenge their owners, just as there are teens who offer to do chores and accept adults' decisions. However, these angelic dogs (and teens) are the exception to the rule, not the norm.

Leadership in Question

First of all, it is important to understand that physical dominance is not leadership. If you use physical and verbal punishments to keep your shepherd in line, it's almost a guarantee that you have not established yourself as first in command. Rather, you've created a combative relationship in which the shepherd will constantly be looking for an opportunity to put an end to all the callous handling. Unfortunately, a shepherd that has acted out against an abusive owner usually ends up in the pound.

A positive relationship between dog and human is a partnership in which the shepherd and handler trust each other implicitly. The owner makes the rules of the house very clear, and those rules do not change. The shepherd knows that if he crosses the line, he will not be rewarded. He may be isolated from his owner and put in a time out for serious offenses; for less serious ones, he will be asked to perform the correct behavior several times and receive rewards. The bottom line is that the shepherd *wants* to work for his owner. His natural inclination is to please his owner; as this person, all you have to do is provide steady, consistent guidance. Working at obedience training every day is a very effective way of reinforcing leadership. There is no need for physical punishment or harsh confrontation.

You can also reinforce your leadership by participating in sports that both you and the dog enjoy, such as agility, fetch (with rules to "give" on command), and hiking. Training for sports provides many opportunities to reward your shepherd for doing the right thing, and it allows you to see how truly gifted your shepherd is.

Nothing for Free

One practice that is extremely effective in establishing and maintaining leadership is making your shepherd work for treats, meals, and affection from you. If she doesn't get anything for free, she will always look to you to know what she should and should not be doing.

 **Fact**

The most difficult part of the "nothing for free" method is convincing smaller children to participate and follow the rules. If you supervise your children's interactions with the dog at all times, you can help them remain consistent in their interactions with her. If children perform these tricks with the dog often, they will soon be viewed as leaders, too.

The way this method works is that before you dole out rewards (body rubs, verbal praise, play rewards, or snacks), the shepherd *must* do something for you or your family. For example, your shepherd could be asked to sit before she receives a biscuit. She might be asked to do a series of actions, such as a sit, down, sit, before jumping up for the treat at the end. When it's feeding time, ask the shepherd to lie down and stay while you put the bowl on the floor. Then let her eat using a release command. She will consider the dinner her reward.

Dealing with Dominant Dogs

Since dogs consider physical attention such as rubs, pats, and scratches as a reward, it is important that the shepherd be required to do something for you to receive this reward. Again, it can be something very, very simple, such as a sit. If you want to work even more on cementing the number-one (you) and number-two (dog) positions, require your shepherd to perform long downs periodically throughout the day or during dinner. Dogs perceive the down position as a sign of submission. Dogs that seek to please their owners will be happy to perform a down, while very dominant dogs can be very resistant to do so. If you have a controlling dog, begin by working on shorter down-stays and work up to down-stays lasting as long as ten, twenty, or thirty minutes.

Here are a few examples of possible situations you could encounter with your dominant shepherd, as well as suggested solutions:

- **Situation:** Your shepherd is lying on the floor and won't get up and out of your way.
  Solution: Slowly shuffle your feet until you come in contact with the dog, and then gently push her until she moves.
- **Situation:** Your shepherd won't get off the couch when you want to sit down.
  Solution: Use a food lure to move the dog. Work on the "Off" command for future use.
- **Situation:** Your shepherd snarls when bumped in bed.
  Solution: Demote the dog to the floor.

Changes in Pack Order

A huge part of maintaining your leadership role with your shepherd is being confident in yourself. It's easy to be comfortable around a puppy. If a puppy talks back to you, it's not intimidating enough to interfere with what you are doing. However, when a full-grown shepherd growls, it can scare off even the most authoritative owner.

It is very important to maintain your stature in front of your dog. If you show even the slightest hint of fear of your shepherd, he's going to pick up on this immediately and walk all over you. If you do feel afraid, think hard about why this is. He is the puppy that you have raised for the last sixteen months. Unless the dog has an unstable temperament or is very aggressive toward people, the shepherd is just trying to intimidate you. If he succeeds in this, all he has to do in the future is growl a little to get his way. You cannot allow him to take advantage of you and change the pack order.

 **Alert!**

Small children and elderly or frail family members who adored the puppy when he was little may be fearful of the big, adult dog. Your shepherd will pick up on this and use it to his advantage. Supervise all interactions between family members and the dog. Focus on command work with the nervous family member and the dog to raise the person's confidence.

Unfortunately, growls can become snaps, which can escalate into bites. If you are having a confidence problem with your shepherd, contact a professional trainer or behaviorist immediately for help. If your shepherd is suddenly exhibiting odd, unpredictable, and aggressive behaviors, first contact your veterinarian. Behaviors that come on suddenly often have a medical cause. After illnesses can be ruled out, consult with an experienced trainer or behavior-ist for assistance.

Dog/Dog Aggression

Most people consider dog/dog aggression something that a domi-nant, controlling, canine bully instigates, but this is not necessarily true. A shepherd that is fearful around other dogs—or perhaps was picked on as a puppy—will often try to set up a good offense (such as lunging, growling, barking, or jumping up on his hind legs to look bigger) to avoid a confrontation with another dog. The manner in which you work with your dog to overcome this antiso-cial behavior depends on whether your dog's aggression is fear-based or control-based.

Fear-Based Aggression

If your shepherd's dog/dog aggression is fear based, you'll notice a difference in the dog's body language just before he reacts to the sight of another dog. He may back up slightly or lean into you. You might see the hair in his ruff rise in an effort to make himself appear bigger. His ears could shift backward, too.

Ways to help your shepherd overcome his fears include the following:

- Maintain a distance at which your shepherd feels he is not threatened by other dogs.
- Divert your dog's attention away from other dogs by giving him something to do. Ask for an on-leash recall, a quick heel, jump for a treat, or start jogging. Always reward good behavior.
- Walk your shepherd with another dog that is confident and friendly. Timid dogs can learn a lot from outgoing friends.
- Work on confidence-building sports. The more confidence your shepherd has in himself, the less frightened he will be of other dogs.

- Practice obedience with a club. Training will give you more control over your shepherd, and club members will be able to help you, too.

Control-Based Aggression

If your shepherd's dog/dog aggression is control based, his entire body will stiffen. He will appear rigid and up on his toes, and he will stare at the other dog with intensity, with his ears forward. He may wag his tail, but this does not indicate friendliness. You might also see his hindquarter drop slightly so that he can lunge forward to attack.

If you own an aggressive shepherd that is not fearful of other dogs, consult with a professional for help. While the fear-based dog-aggressive shepherd will not attack another dog unless he feels there is no other escape, the control-based dog-aggressive shepherd *will* attack and possibly injure or even kill the other dog. If this is your dog, you need to seek help right away.

 **Fact**

Dominant dogs do not like to perform downs. This is a submissive position that makes them feel vulnerable to an attack. If your dog is resistant to performing downs, you should look for other dominant behaviors and evaluate whether or not you need extra help training him.

When walking your shepherd, maintain a safe distance from all other dogs. You do not want your shepherd's leash to provide him with enough leeway to reach and attack another dog. Keep your shepherd in complete control. When you see another dog approaching, put your shepherd in a down-stay. Step on the leash. Reward him only if he remains in the down-stay until you give the release command. Whatever you do, do not shout at your shepherd. This only serves to excite him more.

If you own a male dog, consider neutering him. If you own a female that is terribly dog-aggressive, consult your veterinarian. Spaying a female has the potential to make her more aggressive. Spaying causes the level of female hormones to plummet, leaving primarily testosterone.

Possessive Aggression

When a dog of any age guards a precious possession, the behavior is typically called "possessive aggression." This implies that you are dealing with an aggressive, dominant dog that wants to be in control. Most often, however, the situation is precisely the opposite. Very often it is timid dogs that are constantly having their things taken away by other dogs or humans that will exhibit this possessive behavior.

This behavior should really be known as resource guarding. The dog has found a treasure and doesn't want to give it up. If in the past the dog repeatedly suffered the loss of favorite items, it is only natural that she will reach the end of her rope and start protecting her items.

 **Fact**

A dog can become possessive of something that doesn't seem desirable, such as a tissue, an empty plastic milk jug, or a rubber band. The dog will only perform resource guarding if she considers the item an interesting and limited resource. Her rationale will rarely be clear to you.

The best way to prevent resource guarding from becoming an issue is to work on the "Take it" and "Give it" commands as a game with your dog. Your primary goal is to build her trust in you. She needs to know that you will give the item back. Then when you really must take the item—if it is something that could injure her or is very valuable, for instance—she will willingly give it up. See Chapter 16 for instructions on teaching the "Take it" and "Give it" commands.

Swapping is another method to use when dealing with possessive aggression. If your shepherd has an item she really shouldn't have—but you haven't fully trained her on "Take it" and "Give it"—swap something better for the stolen item. Offer her a tasty treat in exchange for her treasure. Praise her when she drops the thing, and give her the treat. Dispose of the treasure or put it in a place where the shepherd won't find it again.

Territorial Aggression

Guarding your home and yard comes naturally to the shepherd. Serious guarding instincts begin to appear during adolescence, when a previously sweet shepherd transforms almost overnight into a strong-willed protector of the universe.

You do want your shepherd to alert you to anyone approaching your home, as long as he will calm down when you give a "Hush" command. When you let someone in the front door, however, you want the shepherd to turn off his guard instincts and immediately change back into a well-mannered pet. Often, your shepherd *will* behave in this manner if he is well socialized—he won't bark at your guests if he's not afraid of them—as well as well-trained (will remain in a sit-stay if asked) and trusting in you (even if he doesn't approve of your choice of guests).

 Question?

Which is more territorial: a female shepherd or a male shepherd?
There are exceptions to every rule, but in general, male shepherds are more protective of property and female shepherds are more protective of people.

Sometimes when a shepherd hits adolescence, she becomes increasingly territorial. Part of the reason for this is that the adolescent shepherd's owner often thinks he's finished working with his shepherd. He did all the puppy training, housetraining, and a little obedience work—what's left to do? But the shepherd is not like other breeds; she is a lifelong project. If you stop taking her out of the home regularly for socialization, she is apt to become increasingly territorial about her home and yard.

▲ With careful attention, you can curb early signs of aggression in your pet.

A shepherd that is very territorial is difficult to own as a house pet. If the shepherd is protective to the point where only family members can enter the home, life gets complicated. If you want to have friends come over and be safe around the dog, you will have to crate her. She will have to be crated, too, if your children have friends come over to play.

Since confinement to her home seems to increase a shepherd's sense of protection, it would follow that the more you get her out of the house, the less territorial she will be. Actually, this seems to work. The more the shepherd is outside of her home, whether riding in the car, going for a jog, or attending training classes, this time away appears to lessen the dog's territorial behavior.

 **Alert!**

Never chain your shepherd in the yard or put him on a line. The combination of natural territorial protectiveness and the fear of having no escape can create a worried, unstable, and potentially vicious dog. Statistically, chained dogs are the cause of more than one-third of all fatal dog attacks.

Additionally, if your shepherd is an intact male, consider neutering him. Neutering does not alter the dog's basic character, but it does tend to take the testosterone-charged male down a notch. It could help to make the shepherd less territorial. Your dog will still be protective, but his behavior will be more manageable.

Adult Rescue Challenges

The biggest challenge with a developing adult rescue dog concerns aggression. You will feel significantly less comfortable with the dog than if you'd raised him from an eight-week-old puppy. This is mostly because when you bring a rescue dog into your house, you haven't had time to know how this shepherd will react in all situations. In essence, you can't trust him. You will be able to trust him in the future, but he must earn that trust over a period of months.

Likewise, you must earn the trust of your shepherd. He must know that you aren't going to take everything away from him, so he doesn't need to guard his treasures. He needs to be able to trust that you won't put him in any frightening situations with other dogs to overcome any fear-related dog aggression. Most important, for him to accept you as his leader, he must respect you.

Alert!

Behaviorists working with adopted adult dogs warn about the "honeymoon period." Some dogs appear to be perfect companions for four to six weeks, and then something changes. It's as if once they get the lay of the land and feel comfortable in their new homes, they start pushing limits—testing your leadership skills and challenging your authority.

Working with a rescued adult shepherd can be a challenge. Self-confident people who are very in tune with dog nuances and body language will have a much easier time if the adopted dog presents any problems. Often, the shepherd that is up for adoption has already passed through his "difficult" period. In this case, what you see is what you get.

Training the Working Dog

PARTNERING WITH A GERMAN SHEPHERD IS AN incredible experience. If you've ever gone through a basic obedience training class with another breed, prepare to be wowed by your shepherd. This dog possesses the instincts and the intelligence necessary to learn a task very quickly, as well as the desire to work with his handler endlessly.

The Importance of a Job

Training your German shepherd constantly and consistently will provide you with a well-behaved, delightful pet. Training helps you maintain your leadership role, and it is a daily reminder for your dog of his place in the family. As valuable as this training is for you, it is even more valuable for your shepherd. Through training, you are giving him the one thing he desires above all else: a job.

The German shepherd was bred for nearly a century to be a working dog. Whether for herding, serving as a K-9, or working as a service dog for the blind, the German shepherd has always been happiest when he is challenged mentally and physically every day. In today's world, there aren't too many of these canine positions available. You have to think of other ways to occupy your shepherd that work with your schedule.

The German shepherd needs to be kept active at all times. If you don't find something for him to do, he will go looking for something to do. Often, the jobs he gives himself are not ones that you would have assigned, such as landscaping (digging holes in your garden), woodworking (chewing windowsills and table legs), and athletic conditioning (scaling the fence). Training your shepherd to respond to basic commands is a great way to keep control of him and protect your personal belongings and space.

Training Collars

Training collars are available in many different styles, each with a specific purpose. Some collars are initially less appealing than others; however, your choice of collar is based upon your dog's abilities, your past training experience, and the collar you're currently using. From gentlest to severest, your choices include flat buckle collars; expandable clip collars, head collars, martingale collars, nylon and metal choke collars, prong collars, and shock collars.

Buckles and Clips

Most people consider the buckle or clip collar their dog's everyday collar. The collar is usually 1 to 1½ inches wide. Buckle collars have sturdy metal buckles and are almost indestructible. Clip collars are expandable (with a four- to six-inch range) with a plastic clip that fastens the collar shut. Convenient and inexpensive, this collar can grow with a puppy. It has two drawbacks. When the collar is at its tightest adjustment, there is a loop of collar that could catch on a crate, a branch, or another object and strangle the dog. Also, some of the plastic clips are so flimsy that if your shepherd is really straining against it, the clip could break, letting the dog loose.

Buckle and clip collars are recommended for training young puppies. They are gentle, and if training is started at home, when a puppy is only eight weeks old, this collar gives you all the control you need.

Head Collars

When the head collar was first used, it was a favorite among owners whose dogs often took *them* for walks. Specifically, owners of large breed, strong dogs that had never been trained to walk nicely (or dogs that had been adopted and hadn't had any training) benefited significantly from the head collar.

This collar is designed so that wherever the dog's head goes, his body follows. When the shepherd pulls hard, he finds himself facing you. Of course, this is not his intention. He learns quickly that if he wants to go forward, he cannot pull.

 **Essential**

Collars come in several different materials. Nylon webbing, which can be flat or rolled (like a rope), is the least expensive material and can be washed. Decorative cotton fabrics can cover flat, nylon collars. These can be washed, too, but after some time the cotton wears thin. Leather collars are flat or rolled. They're durable and don't rub off the shepherd's coat; however, they are usually the most expensive.

The head collar is comfortable for the dog and does not restrain his mouth in any way. He can eat and drink with the head collar on—as well as bite. This collar does resemble a muzzle, so be prepared to have strangers ask if your dog is "dangerous." If you are considering using the head collar, be sure to find a trainer who is experienced in fitting and training with this collar.

Martingale

A martingale collar is a two-piece collar. The first piece is one to two inches wide and wraps almost all the way around the neck. A short length of chain or a strip of nylon loops through both ends of the neck collar piece and then attaches to a ring, forming a triangle. When the dog pulls against the collar, the chain tightens the collar around the dog's neck.

 **Fact**

Another name for the martingale collar is a hound or greyhound collar. Sight hounds (those that hunt by sight with great speed) typically have very narrow, streamlined heads and wider necks, making it easy for them to slip out of a buckle or clip collar.

This collar doesn't choke the dog because the neck section is wide. The purpose of the collar is just to prevent the dog from backing up out of the collar. For example, if a dog puts on the brakes and you continue walking, attempting to drag your shepherd with you, the dog could slip out of the collar. If you pull hard enough, and if the collar is just loose enough, you can actually pull a fixed collar (buckle or clip) off the shepherd's head.

Choke Collars

Also called training collars, choke collars are made either of rolled nylon or chain links. These collars consist of one long piece with a metal ring at both ends. The collar is pushed through one of the rings to form a loop that tightens when the other ring is pulled. This collar can choke a dog and is never recommended as an everyday collar.

 **Essential**

Training collars are very useful for teaching your dog different commands and skills; however, these collars require a high level of training experience—timing is crucial—and self-control and should never be used except under the strict supervision of an experienced trainer.

A prong collar is constructed similarly to a martingale collar. However, the neck section that goes under the throat consists of metal links with prongs that sink into the dog's coat. The collar is fitted snugly so there is no slack; it cannot be "popped" or suddenly tightened. Though the collar looks painful, the prongs are rounded and only dig into the dog's neck if he pulls hard against the collar. If he walks nicely, the collar causes no pain at all.

Shock Collars

The electronic collar is frequently used in field training with hunting dogs to instantly punish a dog's incorrect behavior from great distances—often 500 yards or more. The collar can be set at a range of shock levels, from a mild buzz to a fairly significant jolt. The handler holds the controls, and the dog wears the collar.

The problem with a shock collar is that the handler may not be able to anticipate the dog's reaction to the jolts. Usually this method proves effective relatively quickly, but an inexperienced handler could overdo the jolts and cause significant pain to the dog, making him fearful and jittery. Also, a dog that gets sick of being shocked could turn against the handler if he figures out the system.

With the advent of positive, reward-based reinforcement training, the need for a shock collar is almost nonexistent. The shock collar, like choke and prong collars, is often misused by owners. Using these training tools incorrectly could have serious repercussions for both the dog and the owner.

Outdated Training Practices

In the past, the methods used to train dogs involved punishing the unwanted behaviors. In other words, the dog learned to perform certain behaviors to avoid pain. If a dog lagged while heeling, when he is expected to trot alongside the handler, he would receive a pop or quick jerk on the choke chain. He would continue receiving pops until he caught up and was in the right place. Once in the correct position, the popping would stop.

Simple exercises, such as the sit, were taught using force. The old maneuver was to pull up on the dog's choke chain while pushing down on his haunches. This is possible on a little puppy, but a full-grown shepherd that is being taught basic obedience for the first time will not respond well. It becomes a battle of strength between the dog and the handler.

Fortunately, dog training has come a long way in recent years. Applying the same concepts that have successfully been used to train dolphins, dog trainers quickly discovered that rewarding correct behaviors worked just as well as punishing incorrect behaviors. This began the shift toward operant conditioning, the system that uses *positive* reinforcement or rewards.

Operant Conditioning

Operant conditioning can go two ways. You can reward or reinforce correct behaviors to extinguish the behaviors you don't want; this is called positive reinforcement. Or you can punish incorrect behaviors so that the dog complies to avoid further pain; this is called negative reinforcement.

Alert!

Unfortunately, pain avoidance training presents an opportunity for abusive handlers to try to justify their mishandling of this very intelligent breed. Shepherd handlers using pain avoidance methods are often guilty of exceptionally harsh, brutal training methods, making pops on the choke chain look like routine training practice.

Both the negative- and the positive-reinforcement training methods are effective. Both methods work quickly with very similar retention rates. Negative reinforcement, however, does nothing to build the human-canine bond. The dog is not completing the tasks because he wants to please you but because he doesn't want to suffer pain. The German shepherd breed instinctually wants to please his handler. When you use negative reinforcement, you deprive the dog of this enjoyment.

As you can imagine, in competitions in which a dog's joyful, enthusiastic performance is required to pass, place, or win, the shepherd that has been trained using primarily positive reinforcements has a far better chance than the dog that is trained using pain avoidance methods.

Primary Reinforcers

There are a couple of words in the dog-training vernacular that you should know. A primary reinforcer is the ultimate or end reward for the dog. For your shepherd, this might be physical praise (a brisk rubbing), treats, or play (tugging on a towel or chasing a tennis ball).

Secondary or Conditioned Reinforcers

A secondary reinforcer is the signal to the shepherd that he did something correctly and that he's going to be rewarded very soon with his favorite primary reinforcer. The most commonly used secondary reinforcer is a short, verbal praise, such as "Yes!" When the shepherd hears "Yes!" he knows he performed the desired behavior correctly. Having received his favorite primary reinforcer immediately after hearing "Yes!" he has been *conditioned* to anticipate that the primary reinforcer is coming.

Fact

Other commonly used secondary reinforcers are a click from a clicker, a toot on a whistle, or a clucking noise. Handlers who are already holding things in their hands and those who lack confidence in their coordination will use a verbal sound or word instead of an item.

What you use as your secondary reinforcer is a matter of personal choice; it depends on your preference and the kinds of training you might be doing with your shepherd. Handlers involved in more advanced sports where complex actions are performed at a distance frequently use clickers, whistles, or other items that can be heard easily. If a shepherd is to be handled by multiple family members, a clicker is often used because it always sounds the same and is consistent no matter what the age or vocal range of the trainer.

Shaping Behaviors

Using positive reinforcers enables the handler to shape a dog's behavior, as opposed to physically enforcing the correct behavior. Because shaping is gentle and nonconfrontational, it works well with dogs of all ages (from puppies to adult shepherds) and all temperaments (from malleable to those with attitude).

You can train your shepherd to perform behaviors through free shaping or by using food lures. Both methods work and can be used to teach different behaviors to the same dog. What method you choose depends largely on the behavior you are trying to shape.

Free Shaping

The idea behind free shaping is to catch the dog in the midst of good behavior. If you want to teach your shepherd to sit, for example, you would wait until he sat on his own. Once he is sitting (not while he's on the way), say "Sit!" Then click and reward. (See Chapter 16 for more information on linking the click with the reward.) Every time you see him sitting, give the command, click, and reward.

When you've practiced this exercise for several days, begin saying "Sit!" as your shepherd is starting to sit. He should know by this time that if he gets his haunches on the floor, he will be rewarded. Once he hits the floor in a sit, click and reward. The next step is to give the command when he's listening and attentive but not in the motion of sitting. When he sits, click and reward. Amazingly, you will find that this whole process—from catching your shepherd sitting to being able to give the sit command at random times—moves very quickly.

~~~ Essential

To simplify training portions of this book, the word click is used to represent any conditioned or secondary reinforcer, such as "Yes!" a whistle, a finger snap, a tongue cluck, or a click on the clicker. The word "reward" refers to the primary reinforcer or the end reward, such as a treat, tug toy, rubbing, or patting.

Food Lures

Some of the behaviors you want to produce in your shepherd occur too infrequently for you to wait around all day for her to do them. For example, if your shepherd seems to be in constant motion, it may be hard to catch her in a sit and use the free-shaping method. Shaping a sit using a food lure might be an easier way to add this behavior to her repertoire.

Face your dog, gently holding her collar with your left hand, and hold a treat in your right hand. Hold your hand with fingers down, and slowly pass the treat from the shepherd's nose, up her muzzle, and over the top of her head. You want your fingers as close to her as possible without touching her. If all goes well, she will rock back, following the motion of your hand, and end up sitting.

As soon as she is in a sit, say "Sit!" Then click and reward. After twelve correct repetitions at this level, step it up by saying "Sit!" as she is sitting. After twelve correct repetitions here, move to holding her collar and saying "Sit!" As long as she is getting it right at least eleven out of twelve times, you can keep adding a little more difficulty. Eventually, you'll be able to have her sit even if she's in the middle of trotting across the lawn. (See the following chapter for more information on teaching the "Sit" command.)

Small Steps to Success

Using the method of primary and secondary reinforcers, every skill is taught in microsteps. The dog learns, slowly but surely, what to do and when to do it. If at any time your shepherd does not perform eleven out of twelve repetitions correctly, go back one level in training the command. This rebuilds the shepherd's confidence. Before you move to the next level, make sure you haven't missed a step. Often this type of training fails because the owner does not think the exercise through and fails to use small-enough increments of difficulty for the dog.

▲ Well-trained German shepherds make fantastic companions.

The key to keeping the exercise increments small enough is increasing only one variable at a time. For example, if you are teaching the sit-stay, you would begin with all the steps to teach the sit until you reached the point at which your shepherd routinely sits on command with no touching and no food lure used. To teach the "stay" part of the exercise, you would first add time.

Stand by your dog and put him in a sit. Give the hand signal—a flat hand, palm out toward the dog's face—and the verbal command "Stay!" Count ten seconds. Click and reward. Release your dog. After every successful set (eleven successes out of twelve tries), add ten seconds to the stay. Work until your shepherd stays for one minute.

Now work on distance. Put your dog in a sit-stay. Take one step to the right and immediately step back to your dog. Click and reward. After eleven successes, add time. Take one step to the right, count ten seconds, and then step back to your dog. Click and reward. Then release. Easy, right?

Finding a Good School and Trainer

There are many great books, videos, and Web sites that offer excellent training information for virtually anything you could imagine teaching your shepherd. However, nothing beats getting this excellent advice from an experienced, approachable trainer—someone who can show you precisely what she wants you to do and how she wants you to do it. If you have any questions, she's there to answer them immediately.

Finding a great trainer who is willing to share her expertise can be difficult. Depending on where you live, you might be able to find several good trainers who use positive, reward-based methods. In other areas, you might not be able to find anyone. If your only option is a trainer who uses pain avoidance methods, books, videos, and Web sites will probably be more helpful.

To help track down a trainer who is comfortable working with German shepherds and who uses positive, reward-based training with shaping, talk to your veterinarian. Usually, she will be able to give you a few referrals. If your breeder is in your area, call him to find out whom he would suggest. Did you adopt a rescue? If so, call the folks you worked with at the rescue or shelter to adopt your shepherd. They should have some good ideas, too.

Question?

Are there any professional organizations that list certified trainers in your area?

The Association of Pet Dog Trainers (APDT) can be contacted for referrals in your area, as well as surrounding areas. You should still call and talk personally to these trainers before you sign up for a class. You will want to make sure that the training techniques of the trainer you chose are appropriate for your shepherd and that you are comfortable with the trainer.

Benefits of a Well-trained Dog

A German shepherd that is given the opportunity to challenge his mind as well as body is a very happy shepherd. The owner who takes the time to give this training to her shepherd is richly rewarded as well.

Solid training makes it easier to continue socializing your shepherd. Practicing even basic obedience commands while on a walk will impress the neighbors and present your shepherd in a much different light. He is the good shepherd, and you are the responsible owner; this is the way a German shepherd and his owner should be seen.

It's also much easier to have a well-trained dog around the house. Training is more work initially, but in the long run, you'll be much better off. Constantly trying to keep up with an unruly, ill-tempered shepherd is no fun—not to mention dealing with the damage he is likely to cause. Training is the key ingredient when it comes to raising a happy shepherd and maintaining a happy family.

CHAPTER 16

Teaching the Basics

GERMAN SHEPHERDS ARE SO INTELLIGENT and eager to learn that there's really no reason why your shepherd—whether a puppy from top bloodlines or a rescued adult—shouldn't be able to achieve a Companion Dog obedience title. The shepherd is one of those rare breeds that in three to four repetitions can learn a skill that would take another dog ten to fifteen repetitions. Even if you don't plan on titling your shepherd, teaching your dog a few basic skills will make her a controllable, well-mannered dog.

Choosing Your Reward System

When choosing the primary reinforcer or reward that you are going to use in training your shepherd, the key is to use something your shepherd absolutely loves. For example, a great reward for the cookie-loving dog would be training treats. If you train your shepherd when she's a little hungry, food becomes a strong motivator. For dogs with a tendency to want to control the handler, portioning the dog's meals throughout the day as rewards is one strategy you can use to maintain your leadership role.

Some German shepherds are crazy about retrieving balls. They will fetch and return a ball for as long as you can throw. Chasing after a ball can be a terrific reward for these dogs—as long as they

are trained to reliably return the ball. If you're worried about tossing a ball (a concern when working close to traffic), consider playing tug with your shepherd. A rolled up hand towel works well, but
if you can get your dog to play tug with the leash, you can do this
between exercises as a quick reward.

🐕 fact

Arson- or accelerant-detection dogs are frequently trained using
food. With these dogs, successful detective work is the only way they
receive their meals. The handler portions the dogs' servings and
rewards them throughout the day for finds. If they don't have the
opportunity to work during the day, the handler will incorporate several training sessions so they can eat.

Making the Connection

For the primary/secondary reinforcer method to work, the dog
has to make the connection between the conditioned reinforcer
and the reward. If you've chosen to use a clicker as your conditioned reinforcer and treats as your reward, you would begin with
a handful of treats in one hand and the clicker in the other. When
the shepherd is looking at you, click and give a treat. No need to say
anything. Your shepherd will make the connection fairly quickly.

Practice making the connection between the click and the
reward. Work on this for several days until is obvious that the
sound of the conditioned reinforcer makes your shepherd seek a
reward. Once you've achieved this, you're ready to start training.

Locations

To give your shepherd the greatest chance of success and the least
chance of failure, you need to keep things simple. For the beginning shepherd, find a quiet place in your home to begin training.

Make sure you're alone with the dog. You don't want children running through the room, a cat jumping on and off a chair, or food cooking on the stove. Limit your distractions, and focus on your dog and his training. Even experienced dogs learning new, advanced skills are ideally trained in a quiet environment that is as free of distractions as possible.

Only when you have mastered a skill with your shepherd in a quiet place can you consider working on the same skill in a busier environment. If you've accomplished a reliable ten-minute down-stay standing twenty feet away, you do not want to go to a noisy soccer field and attempt the same task at the same skill level.

Instead, start training the same task, but from the beginning. For the down-stay, this would mean standing beside your shepherd and putting him in a down-stay, alternating adding distance (one step at a time) and time (thirty-second or one-minute increases). Your shepherd will progress very quickly through these steps. This review work builds his confidence and allows him to succeed even if he is a little distracted in the new location. Eventually, as you continue to increase the difficulty, he will hit a point at which his rate of completing the task correctly begins to drop. If he isn't successful eleven out of twelve times, back up and repeat the previous level before proceeding.

Name

Whether you've brought home a young puppy or adopted an adult dog, you'll need to teach your shepherd her name. This job is relatively easy, and with the use of reinforcers, it moves along even more quickly. To do this, you must first establish the connection between the sound of the conditioned reinforcer and the reward with your shepherd.

Wait until she is looking at you, and say her name: "Sheila!" Click and reward. (This is a good example of using free shaping to teach a behavior.) Repeat this exercise at least twelve times. Then say her name when she is close by and not distracted, when the possibility of her looking at you even without you saying her name is extremely high. When she looks at you, click and reward. Repeat this at least twelve times. Your next step is to add a variable. One variable could be her distance away from you when you say her name. Continue to work on this until you can say your shepherd's name softly from across the room and she will still turn and look at you.

Sit

The sit is perhaps the most useful command in your obedience repertoire. Putting your shepherd on a sit when someone is coming in the front door gives you more control over the situation. Requiring your shepherd to sit while you prepare her dinner is much more convenient than trying to navigate around a dancing shepherd in the kitchen. If your shepherd is in a sit when you put the bowl down, you won't have the bowl knocked out of your hands. Putting your shepherd in a sit is also a convenient way to keep control of the large dog around small children and frail adults.

 **Alert!**

The shepherd learns quickly, which means he will learn both correct behaviors and incorrect behaviors rapidly. As his trainer, you need to be aware of exactly what you are teaching him. If you click at the wrong time on the sit, she could learn that the command "Sit" means crouching on the way to a sit. Training the skill correctly the first time is much easier than trying to fix an incorrectly taught skill.

If you are using free shaping to teach the sit, you'll need to carry your clicker and treats with you around the house. Every time she sits, say "Sit!" and immediately click and reward. When she seems to have made the connection between the command and the sit, give the command "Sit!" as she is beginning to sit. When her rump hits the floor, click and reward.

When she performs this correctly at least eleven out of twelve times, give the command "Sit!" when she is looking at you and making eye contact—but not preparing to sit. Continue to add variables, such as distance, initial positioning (such as when she's already in a down or standing), and movement (when she's walking or standing still).

The sit is also frequently taught using a food lure. Stand facing your shepherd, and gently hold her collar with your left hand to keep her in front of you. Hold a treat in your right hand. Starting at her nose, slowly move the treat (fingers down and wrapped around the treat) above her muzzle and over her head. Your fingers should nearly touch her as your hand moves over her head toward her back.

This lure movement will cause your shepherd to rock back on her haunches. As soon as she plants herself, say "Sit!" click and reward. Repeat this at least twelve times or until she is easily moving into the sit as the lure is moved over her head.

 **Essential**

Don't be surprised if your shepherd begins sitting when she would like a treat. She may also glance back and forth between you and the treat jar to initiate a quick training session. This is okay—shepherds love to perform for their humans. Just be sure that you ultimately remain in control.

Next, give the command "Sit!" as she is rocking back with the movement of the food lure. As soon as she sits, click and reward. When she is consistent at this skill level, give the command when you are holding the treat. She should sit. If she does, click and reward. If she doesn't sit, go back to giving the command while moving the food lure over her head. Work until she is completing this correctly eleven out of twelve times.

Down

The down can be used in the home for the same purposes as the sit. As far as usefulness, the down runs a close second to the sit. The down is also a submissive position that can be used when working with a dog-aggressive shepherd while out on walks, or in the home with an adult dog that is having issues with authority.

The down can be taught using the free-shaping method. If you are using a food lure, you want to make sure that the down is shaped correctly. Often, handlers teach the down from the sit position. This results in a dog that sits first and then lies down on the "Down" command. You want to teach the down while your shepherd is standing. From this position, the shepherd will hit the ground going down in the front first and then the rear. Teaching this method allows you to achieve snappy downs while your shepherd is in motion. Besides helping you maintain control of the dog, it is guaranteed to impress your friends and neighbors.

Question?

Are there any professional organizations that list certified trainers in your area?

The Association of Pet Dog Trainers (APDT) can be contacted for referrals in your area, as well as surrounding areas. You should still call and talk personally to these trainers before you sign up for a class. You will want to make sure that the training techniques of the trainer you chose are appropriate for your shepherd and that you are comfortable with the trainer.

When your shepherd is standing, hold her gently by the collar with one hand and have a treat in the other hand. Move the treat slowly down her chest as you progress farther into and under her. She should fold into a down. As soon as she is all the way down, say "Down!" click and reward. If your shepherd is a bit dominant, she may resent being put into this compromising position. Keep working on her. When she finds that good things happen to her when she obediently goes into a down (and nothing happens when she doesn't), she will become more accommodating.

If you are having a particularly difficult time getting your shepherd to fold into a down—if she starts talking to you (rumbling, growling, or snarling), seek professional help immediately. Under a good trainer's guidance, you will get past this obstacle.

Go to Your Place

When you are eating, it can be quite annoying to have your shepherd sitting right next to you, watching every forkful move from the plate to your mouth. For this reason, the "Go to your place" command is very useful during meals. This command instructs your dog to lie down on a designated mat or in her crate and stay there. If your shepherd's place is a mat, you'll be able to take this mat anywhere (such as a friend's house or a training class) and have her lie and stay in this spot.

The "Go to your place" command involves a series of actions linked together. To teach a sequence of actions, start with the final action and work your way backwards through the chain. Therefore, if you are using the free-shaping method, you would begin by giving the command "Go to your place" while your shepherd is already in her crate or lying on the mat you'd like to use. Click and reward.

If she's not freely offering this behavior, use a food lure. Start with her standing on the mat and say, "Down." Click and reward. Repeat. Next, add the motion to the mat. Have her stand next to you on leash (but not under a command). The mat should not be more than one step directly in front of you. Use your food lure to move her forward to the mat. As soon as all four of her feet are on the mat, give the command "Go to your place!" Click and reward. Repeat this several times. Next, give the command when she is moving onto the mat but only has her front two paws on it. As soon as all four paws are on the mat, click and reward. Repeat this several times. Then give the command when she is standing directly in front of the mat. As soon as all four paws are on the mat, click and reward. Repeat this step several times.

Once your shepherd performs these steps successfully, reintroduce the down. This time, begin the exercise with your shepherd standing directly in front of the mat. Say, "Go to your place!" As soon as all four paws are on the mat, say, "Down!" (without a click). When she hits the mat in a down, immediately click and reward. Repeat this over and over.

Now, as you see her anticipating the "Down!" begin fading out this command. That is, allow her to go into the down without waiting for your command. Click and reward. Repeat. At this point, you can start adding distance back into the exercise, working a step at a time.

Wait and Stay

The "Wait" command is helpful when letting an anxious, dirty-pawed puppy out of his crate or when keeping a full-grown shepherd from jumping out of the car until you can snap on a leash. If you're taking your shepherd for a walk and he tends to bound down the porch steps much faster than you, you can tell him to wait so that you can walk down the steps at your leisure.

With your puppy or adult in his crate, barely open the door and hold your shepherd back. Give the command "Wait," then click and reward. Shut the crate door. Repeat this, opening and shutting the crate door with each repetition. Work on opening the door wider and wider.

Essential

The "Wait" is slightly different from the "Stay" command. Your shepherd will know that "Wait" means a temporary pause, whereas "Stay" means he must not move until further notice.

As you feel that you are no longer holding the shepherd and that he is waiting, try this without your hand on him. This time, open the crate just a little and put up your hand in a "Stop" position, as if you were a traffic director. Click and reward. Repeat. Increase how wide you open the crate door with each successful set of repetitions. Eventually, you should be able to tell your shepherd to wait, open his crate door all the way, walk across the room, and come back to release him.

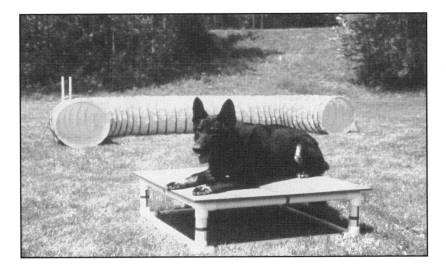

▲ The "Stay" command is an important one and should be mastered as early as possible.

The "Stay" command can be taught as a sit-stay, a down-stay, or a stand-stay. Typically, the sit or down is the most comfortable position to begin the stay. In the following example, the sit-stay is used.

Put your shepherd in a sit. Give the command "Stay!" Wait ten seconds. Click and reward. Repeat. Increase the duration of the stay until you have reached one minute. Now, begin adding distance. Put him in a sit next to you. Give him the command "Stay!" Take one step to the right and immediately step back. Click and reward. Repeat this several times.

 Fact

Dogs are very visual creatures, and they learn hand signals even faster than they learn verbal commands. To introduce a hand signal for any command, give the signal when you say the verbal command. Then fade out the verbal command—say the command every other repetition—while continuing to use the hand signal.

From this point, you can either add more distance (two steps and immediately back to him) or time (one step away, hold ten seconds, step back). Click and reward. Repeat. Make sure he performs at least eleven out of twelve repetitions correctly in each set before increasing the time or distance variables.

Come

Since many shepherds find ways to get loose at one time or another, this command could save your dog's life. If your shepherd romps near a busy street and she won't come when you call her, the results could be fatal. A solid recall, however, will allow you to let your shepherd off the leash in public areas, such as beaches and dog parks.

When teaching the recall or the "Come" command, the most important rule to remember is that everything should be performed on leash. The reason for this is simple: You're setting your shepherd up for success by not allowing any opportunity for her not to come. You can begin this command while on walks by randomly walking backwards. When your shepherd wheels around to change direction, say "Come!" Click and reward, and practice this again and again.

🐕 Alert!

If your shepherd is loose and her selective hearing is irritating you, be careful how you respond when she does come. If you scold her for running around, she will learn that "Come" means "If I go to you now, I'm going to get in trouble." It will take at least twenty good recalls to return her to her previous recall proficiency level.

Next, you can put her on a sit-stay in front of you and say "Come" as you're trotting backwards. Your shepherd will bounce after you. Click and reward, and practice, practice, practice. Add distance by standing a step back from your shepherd's sit-stay before you begin running backwards. Click and reward, and continue practicing. When you have reached the point at which you are calling your shepherd from the end of the leash, you can drop the backwards running. As your shepherd runs to you, click and reward.

From this point, you'll want to purchase a long leash—twenty feet or more. Work on building distance and continue to encourage a swift, enthusiastic recall. Only use the "Come" command when your shepherd is on leash or when she is already running straight for you. If you use this command to bring your shepherd in from the backyard before she is solid on it, you run a substantial risk of her not coming—which could move you back weeks in your training.

Walk Nicely

Somewhere between four and eight months of age, your puppy will gain a substantial amount of size and strength. If you haven't taught him the basics of walking nicely on a leash by this time, he's likely walking you. If you adopted an adult dog, he may or may not have had experience on a leash. An adult dog can pull exceptionally hard, making him difficult to control.

One way to work with a puppy or an adult dog that pulls is to reverse or change direction suddenly without saying anything. Your neighbors will likely think you are nuts for walking in bizarre patterns; however, your shepherd will learn that if he pulls and isn't paying attention, he'll feel a tug on the leash and have to catch up with you.

 **Fact**

Using a head collar allows anyone to be able to walk a strong adult shepherd with pulling tendencies. With this collar, as soon as the dog pulls, his body whips around to follow his head, causing him to stop. He quickly learns that pulling doesn't move him forward.

Additionally, while working with your shepherd on good leash manners, always reward good behavior. Whenever he is in a good position, click and reward. If you want precision heeling from your shepherd, you will continue to refine this position while walking straight ahead for short distances (such as ten yards). The variables to increase will be distance and direction. Remember to introduce variables one at a time and in small increments.

Take It and Give It

German shepherds frequently steal back favorite toys or food items they don't want to part with. Can you blame them? How upset would you be if someone reached over and took your cell phone while you were in the middle of a phone call? But how would you feel if someone you knew and trusted asked to borrow the cell phone for just a minute and promised to return it? The same logic applies to your shepherd.

Fact

Allow your shepherd to keep the toy at the end of most sessions. If you don't allow her to keep the item, give her a jackpot (a whole handful of treats) for allowing you to keep the item. This will build her trust in you.

The ability to have your shepherd give you an item on command is based on the dog's trust in you. The way you build up this trust is through practice. Begin with the "Take it" portion of this exercise by asking your shepherd to hold an item for you. The item should be a toy she enjoys but doesn't steal. When she takes the toy you've offered in her mouth, give the command "Take it." Click and reward. (She will drop the toy for the treat.) Practice this repeatedly. Repeat this exercise again, but this time give the command as she is opening her mouth. Click when she has taken the item, reward her, and practice this until she is taking the item when it's offered to her.

When your shepherd drops the item she's holding for the treat, give the command "Give it." Click, reward her, and practice repeatedly. When she's reliably releasing the item for the treat, give the command while she is holding the item. When she drops it for you, click and reward. Use different items with different textures so that she associates this exercise with a variety of different items.

CHAPTER 17

Basic Dog Health Care

RAISING A HEALTHY PUPPY and maintaining an adult dog's good health involve feeding the right foods, giving your shepherd sufficient exercise and mental stimulation, and providing him with excellent veterinary care. Preventive veterinary care is perhaps the most effective way to improve and extend your German shepherd's life. This is definitely a situation in which $25 or $30 spent today could save you hundreds tomorrow.

Holistic Versus Conventional Veterinary Medicine

Conventional veterinary medicine is most likely the type of care you are used to providing for your pets. The conventional veterinary practitioner prescribes medications, uses the latest diagnostic tools, and follows peer-reviewed studies that could impact or change the way she treats certain injuries or illnesses.

Veterinarians may specialize in a certain aspect of medicine, in much the same way a physician may choose to specialize in neurology or obstetrics. Veterinarians who complete at least three years of postgraduate studies in a special area of interest must undergo a peer review before they can receive the title of diplomate from various prestigious professional veterinary medicine organizations, such as the American College of Veterinary Behaviorists (ACVB).

Holistic veterinary medicine includes such unconventional modalities as acupuncture, chiropractic, homeopathy, flower essences, raw diets, nutraceuticals (the use of concentrated doses of vitamins, minerals, and enzymes to treat disease), Chinese medicine, and herbs. The holistic veterinarian is trained and has received her veterinary medicine degree (DVM) from a veterinary college that teaches conventional medicine.

Some holistic veterinarians combine conventional and holistic modalities. For example, a holistic veterinarian may utilize the latest diagnostic tools, from MRIs to specific blood and urine tests, as well as practice acupuncture. Another holistic veterinarian may dedicate her entire practice to homeopathy—the practice of treating diseases with very dilute, pure forms of compounds that if ingested in a concentrated form would cause the same symptoms as the disease being treated—and not use any conventional medicine.

Whether you choose to go to a veterinarian with a conventional, holistic, or combined practice, you'll want to find a professional who is not only skilled but who is also accessible. A veterinarian could be the most experienced, awarded, and titled individual in the country, but if you don't feel comfortable asking questions, all of this veterinarian's expertise is wasted. You and your shepherd can't benefit from veterinary care unless you can freely communicate with your veterinarian.

Finding a Veterinarian

If you've had dogs in the past and have worked with a veterinarian in your area, you're lucky. You don't have to search for veterinary care. If you are a first-time dog owner or if you're new to your area, you'll need to find someone to work with—preferably before your shepherd comes home.

🐕 Alert!

Breeders' contracts often require you to get a veterinary examination within forty-eight to seventy-two hours of your purchase of the dog. If you haven't selected your veterinarian prior to purchasing a puppy, you might not be able to schedule an examination within this time period.

Usually, if you've adopted your shepherd from a local rescue, you will be given a list of preferred veterinarians. These are trusted veterinarians with whom individuals from the rescue have had experience. If you've purchased a puppy from a local breeder, she most likely has some veterinarians to recommend as well.

You can also check with the local animal shelters and humane societies. Certain veterinarians in the community donate or discount their services to shelters so that these shelters will have more money to care for and place animals. These veterinarians are often highly skilled, in addition to having their hearts in the right place.

When searching for a veterinarian, take into consideration where the veterinarian is located; in an emergency, you'll appreciate someone who's right around the corner. You should also find out how much she charges for routine exams, how she handles after-hours emergencies, and in what areas her interest and expertise lie. If she primarily treats exotic pets, you might feel more comfortable with someone who specializes in dogs. Even better is a veterinarian who specializes in dogs and genuinely likes German shepherds.

If costs are a concern to you, you might want to investigate the private practitioner's clinic. This professional often does not have the overhead (hospital, staff, expensive radiograph and MRI equipment, and multiple surgical suites) of larger animal hospitals, which means she'll likely have lower rates. Depending on the needs you anticipate for your dog, this option may be just fine.

Unfortunately, no one can anticipate an emergency. It's usually not a matter of *if* you and your shepherd will have a veterinary crisis, but *when*. An animal hospital may be able to provide round-the-clock care, whereas a clinic may have to refer you to an emergency facility. Both services may be excellent; it could be a matter of what you are comfortable with, given that the emergency clinic will not have your dog's records on hand; potential expenses, as independent emergency veterinary hospitals tend to charge high rates; and location. If an emergency clinic is halfway across town, it may not be a practical alternative.

Preventive Veterinary Medicine

Puppies will require multiple veterinary exams, vaccinations, and preventive medications in their first year. An adult dog may not require as much preventive veterinary medical care as a puppy; however, there are several preventive measures that need to be taken to ensure the best quality of life possible for your shepherd.

Too often, owners fall into a false sense of security when their dogs are young because there aren't many problems. But without early and continued care to prevent disease, your shepherd runs a higher risk of becoming ill. Many of the diseases and parasites that can be crippling or even fatal are avoidable with today's veterinary medical care and general knowledge of how these diseases are transmitted.

Vaccinations

The age group that is most susceptible to potentially fatal viruses and diseases is young puppies. For this reason, puppies are typically given a series of combined vaccines over a period of up to four months of age. The vaccinations begin at six weeks of age and are given every two to three weeks, continuing until the shepherd is fourteen to sixteen weeks old.

The frequency with which your puppy receives his vaccinations will depend on the risk of specific diseases in your area.

Vaccinations are usually finished by the time the puppy is fourteen to sixteen weeks old; however, your veterinarian may choose to give your shepherd one additional vaccination. Some research indicates that the German shepherd may not be able to produce the necessary antibodies to fight off disease until a later age.

▲ A little outdoor play will help dull the sting of a vaccination.

Initially, antibodies are passed on to the puppies through the mother. The mother's antibodies may stop protecting the puppy as early as six weeks of age. The moment this happens, the puppy is susceptible to several fatal diseases. At this point, the puppy should receive his first set of vaccinations. If his mother's antibodies are no longer circulating in his body, the vaccination will cause his body to react and produce its own antibodies.

If the puppy still has antibodies from his mother, the vaccination won't work. This is why puppies receive a series of vaccinations. The veterinarian has no way of knowing when the puppy is susceptible to disease, so by giving the vaccinations every few weeks, she is hoping to catch the puppy as soon as he is receptive to the vaccinations.

Alert!

An adopted adult dog will usually receive two doses of the combined vaccine, rather than the entire series of combined vaccinations as a puppy would. Most adult dogs receive their vaccinations every one to three years, depending on the type of vaccination used and for what diseases.

Core Vaccines

The puppy's series of vaccines include canine distemper, canine parvovirus, canine hepatitis, and canine influenza. These vaccines are usually bundled together as a combined vaccination, so your shepherd will only have to undergo one needle prick instead of four. When your puppy is between fourteen and sixteen weeks old, he will receive an individual rabies vaccination, followed by a rabies booster shot at one year of age.

Adults receive only one dose of the combined vaccination. These vaccines were previously developed for annual use. In 2004, however, a combination vaccination became available that is proven to protect the dog for three years. If there is no information on when your adopted adult received his last rabies vaccination, he will need to get one. Depending on where you live, your shepherd may be required to receive additional rabies vaccinations annually or every three years.

Additional Vaccines

Core vaccinations are those that protect your shepherd from diseases that are known to be highly contagious and life threatening. Unless there are extenuating circumstances, your veterinarian will recommend that these vaccinations be given every three years. But your veterinarian may strongly recommend that your shepherd receive additional vaccines, too.

The vaccine for bordetella (kennel cough) is required if you plan to board your dog at a commercial facility. It is also highly recommended if you travel with your dog or attend events where large groups of dogs are present. If you live near bodies of water such as rivers, streams, creeks, or lakes and you spend time with your dog outside, your veterinarian may recommend a vaccination to prevent the protozoan giardia from infesting your shepherd. For those living on working farms, or who might visit with their working shepherds, the leptospirosis vaccination may be recommended. Dogs may become infected with leptospirosis if they are exposed to stagnant water, come in contact with wild animal or cattle urine, or eat food that has been contaminated by rats carrying the disease.

Essential

Some dogs have adverse reactions to vaccinations, ranging from minor discomfort to anaphylaxis. Watch your shepherd carefully after he receives a vaccination and see your veterinarian immediately if you notice any swelling, redness, or tenderness, or an abscess at the site of the injection. Possible reactions that require urgent care include tremors, seizures, and swelling around the throat, face, and tongue.

A tickborne disease that is spreading across the United States is Lyme disease. Currently, dogs in the Northeast, mid-Atlantic region, Midwest, and even some states in the Southwest are at risk of coming in contact with ticks infected with this disease. These ticks are tiny, and very often owners never even realize that their dogs have been bitten. Lyme disease is serious. If not prevented through vaccines or treated immediately after infection, it can cause lasting side effects.

Fleas and Ticks

Because of the shepherd's thick double coat, it can be difficult to spot a few fleas or ticks, even if you are brushing your dog on a regular basis. Fleas will multiply until they begin to leave telltale flea dirt, which is flea excrement. By the time you spot this, you'll likely be dealing with a sizeable infestation. The fleas will have dropped their eggs throughout your home and in the dog's bed.

Signs that your shepherd may have fleas are itching, scratching, and rubbing. The German shepherd is a breed that is more likely to have allergic reactions to fleabites than many other breeds. All it takes is one bite to cause a puppy or dog with this allergy to suffer from inflammation; red, raw skin; open lesions; uncomfortable itching; and chronic ear infections. Even if your shepherd isn't allergic, fleas carry several different infectious diseases, as well as the infectious larval stage of various parasitic worms.

Ticks are not any better. Lyme disease is just one of the diseases carried by ticks. The sites of tick bites can become infected and can also cause unpleasant skin reactions in the shepherd. Ticks are especially hard to locate, due to their minute size, and they burrow into the skin, making them even more difficult to spot.

 Fact

The flea and tick repellent, Frontline Top Spot, contains fipronil. In a recent study, fipronil showed effectiveness in preventing a tick carrying Lyme disease from infecting the canine host. This product could possibly make vaccinations for Lyme disease obsolete.

Fortunately, fleas and ticks do not have to be a problem. You no longer have to go through your shepherd's coat with a flea comb from spring to fall (year-round in warmer climates), use chemical flea dips and dusting powders, or purchase flea collars. And you won't have to continually check favorite tick locations (tails, ears, and other areas where the blood supply is close to the skin's surface) to pick off these parasites by hand.

Your veterinarian can prescribe oral products that repel fleas and ticks, or topical solutions that are applied to the dog's skin, which kill fleas and ticks before they can transmit diseases. If applied according to the manufacturers' directions, it is possible for your shepherd to go through a whole summer without a single bite from a flea or tick.

Internal Parasites

The very idea of an infestation of worms in a puppy or an adult shepherd is pretty disgusting. Some worms, such as the tapeworm, are relatively asymptomatic in healthy dogs, meaning the dog's health does not noticeably suffer as a result of infestation. But other worms cause serious illness, such as roundworms, whipworms, and hookworms. Still other worms can be lethal if not prevented or treated immediately.

Heartworms

The most lethal of all worms, and the parasite with which most owners are familiar, is heartworm. Heartworm is not transmitted through feces, urine, or vomit. Rather, a mosquito carrying heartworm larvae must bite a dog, injecting the larvae into the dog's blood. Once in the dog's bloodstream, the larvae migrate to the dog's heart, where adult worms may grow from six to twelve inches long. In addition to taking up residence in the heart, heartworms may also live in pulmonary arteries and major veins supplying the heart.

If left untreated, heartworms may cause congestive heart failure or renal failure. The treatment for ridding a dog of these worms is lengthy and not without risks, so preventing heartworms is the easiest way to keep your shepherd safe. Heartworm medications can be given orally on a daily or monthly basis.

Intestinal Worms

Virtually all German shepherds will have intestinal worms at some point in their lives. The intestinal worms that cause the most trouble are roundworms, whipworms, and hookworms. Tapeworms can also be problematic, but the infestation must be quite heavy or the overall health of the infected shepherd quite frail for infestation by this parasite to have serious implications.

 **Alert!**

Most puppies are born with roundworm because the larval stage of these worms is passed to the puppies from their mothers. For this reason, breeders worm their pups at two, four, six, and eight weeks of age. It's your job to have your veterinarian continue these dewormings at ten and twelve weeks.

Roundworms are most frequently seen in puppies and cause a puppy's belly to appear distended. Though the pups look like they're full and plump, they are actually quite ill. If the roundworms are not eradicated, the pups will become malnourished and emaciated. The larvae from these worms can migrate to the puppy's lungs, which causes coughing. Other symptoms of an infestation are diarrhea, vomiting, a rough-textured coat, and underdeveloped muscling.

Ingesting the fecal matter or vomit of an infected dog transmits hookworms. Adult hookworms attach to the lining of the intestines and can cause anemia, vomiting, and chronic bloody diarrhea. The same dewormer that is effective in overcoming roundworms is effective in getting rid of hookworms.

Whipworms attach themselves to the dog's colon and cause bloody diarrhea, vomiting, and severe weight loss. Though a dewormer is effective in ridding the dog of whipworms, it is very easy for the dog to become infested again. The larvae from whipworms can live up to thirty-five days or longer, while adult worms have a lifespan of up to sixteen months. Eggs are shed through fecal matter and can re-infect your shepherd. Careful, daily pickup of all fecal matter in the yard is required to reduce the chance of this happening.

Question?

Isn't there any way to prevent your shepherd from getting worms in the first place?
Yes. Infestations of roundworms, hookworms, and whipworms can be prevented entirely by giving your shepherd one of several heart-worm preventives on a regular schedule.

Tapeworms are the largest of the blood ingesting intestinal worms. With lengths of up to several feet, depending on the type of tapeworm, you would think that these worms would be more devastating than they actually are. In fact, puppies and adults with tapeworms are often asymptomatic. A very heavy infestation of tapeworms may cause slight weight loss, a decrease in appetite, and a dull coat—but usually these symptoms are not obvious.

Often, tapeworms are discovered either by the owner spotting sections of tapeworms in the dog's feces or through an annual, routine fecal exam with the veterinarian. Tapeworms are easily eradicated using a dewormer.

Emerging Diseases and Concerns

Though West Nile virus has recently been watched for its impact on dogs, to date only a handful of dogs with the virus have died— though the virus was not necessarily the cause of death. A vaccine has been produced for horses, a species that is acutely affected by the virus. However, no vaccine has been developed for canines; at this time, there is not a need for one.

🐕 Alert!

Many dogs across the country did become ill or die because of the panic surrounding West Nile virus. Owners were applying mosquito repellent with DEET to their dogs, which is quite poisonous when ingested and proved to be fatal to a significant number of dogs.

Researchers continue to keep an eye on this virus and many others. Viruses frequently mutate to survive. Parvovirus is one such example. The vaccine for this virus has undergone several modifications to account for these changes and to make sure that the antibodies produced by the dog could fight off the newest version of the disease.

Additionally, though uncommon, viruses do cross species. In 2004, for example, an equine virus mutated and infected a large population of racing greyhounds in Florida. The virus was contained, but it is easy to see how a disease can unexpectedly jump from one species to another.

In addition to altered viruses, the danger of foreign diseases traveling from countries around the world and infecting dogs in the United States is quite possible. With the speed of air travel, it is feasible for an infected host to survive the flight and potentially find a new host here. It's certainly not something to lose sleep over; however, it's good to be aware that diseases are not static and that they will mutate, travel, or cross species to improve their chances of surviving.

Emergencies

Accidents can happen virtually anywhere: at home, at the park, or while traveling. It is very important that you keep your veterinarian's phone number displayed in an obvious spot in your home, preprogrammed in your cell phone, and on a slip of paper in your wallet. If your shepherd suffers a serious injury or is suddenly overcome by heat stroke, you can call to alert your veterinarian that you are on the way and receive valuable first-aid advice while in the car.

Additionally, keep the number for the after-hours clinic posted in the same places. Your shepherd's emergencies could very well occur in the middle of the night when your regular veterinarian is not available.

 **Essential**

When stressed, you may not be able to think rationally. If you are trying to figure out where the emergency veterinary clinic is while you are attempting to apply pressure to your shepherd's bleeding wound, there's a good chance you'll get lost. Take a practice drive to the clinic during daylight hours so that you are familiar with the route.

Some owners are able to lift and carry their adult shepherds to the car—the German shepherd is a large dog. If you don't think you can lift your dog, roll him onto a blanket, and with the help of someone else, lift the four corners and carry the dog to the car in this sling. If you don't have anyone to assist you, the worst-case scenario is that you have to drag the blanket to the car and summon all your strength for the final lift.

When dogs are in pain, their natural reaction is to bite—don't take it personally. If you are concerned that your shepherd may snap or might bite someone who is helping you, muzzle him while you are lifting him and carrying him to the car. You can use a long sock, pantyhose, or even a tie to make a temporary muzzle. Begin with the length of material on top of the dog's muzzle. Cross the fabric under his jaw, back up to the top of his nose and cross again. Finally, tie it behind his ears. As soon has you have him loaded, take off the tie. It's difficult for him to breathe with a tied muzzle, and if he is in pain, he will likely be panting.

Advanced Care

I N ADDITION TO PROVIDING YOUR SHEPHERD with the best in preventive veterinary care, you should be aware of several diseases, conditions, and injuries that tend to be particularly problematic for the German shepherd. Armed with this knowledge, you can be on the lookout for symptoms that could indicate that your shepherd needs immediate, veterinary attention. Regardless of the disease, condition, or injury involved, the sooner your shepherd receives veterinary care, the better her chances of recovering.

German Shepherd Diseases

When it comes to diseases, there are some that are infectious—a shepherd can catch these from any infected dog. These are primarily the viruses and parasitic infections listed in Chapter 17. A German shepherd may also develop a condition in utero called a congenital defect or disease. The defect is present at birth; however, the effects may not appear for years. Some congenital defects are believed to be hereditary.

Hereditary diseases, those that can be passed from one generation to another, are of great concern to shepherd breeders. These are the diseases for which breeders test (if possible), and certify that their dogs are free of before they are allowed to breed.

The problem with some hereditary diseases is that a dog may not show symptoms of having the disease until she has already been bred several times. These late-appearing hereditary diseases are the most difficult to eradicate. Reputable breeders try to keep accurate records and track these diseases in their lines to determine how to eliminate the disease.

Fatal Diseases

Though many German shepherd diseases are chronic or recurring, few turn out to be the actual cause of death among the breed. For example, older German shepherds frequently suffer from osteoarthritis. The condition can become so painful that the shepherd is no longer mobile, even with medications. At this point, the kindest route may be to euthanize the dog to relieve her of the pain. In this case, the arthritis itself didn't kill her, but the arthritis was the reason behind her death.

The life-threatening diseases that are specific to or found in significantly higher rates in the German shepherd population include several forms of heart disease and at least two very aggressive forms of cancer: hemangiosarcoma and osteosarcoma. Additionally, nodular dermatofibrosis (a skin-related condition) is more commonly seen in the German shepherd than in other breeds. Though the skin disease is not fatal, dogs suffering from this disease invariably develop either malignant kidney tumors (cystadenocarcinoma) or cancers of the uterus (in females that have not been spayed).

Other Areas of Concern

The German shepherd tends to be more susceptible to unexplained diarrhea (no determined cause), lameness or a weak limb (no known cause), heavy flea infestations, ear infections, compulsive disorders (spinning and tail chasing), degenerative myelopathy (loss of function in the pelvic limbs), and ruptured cranial cruciate ligaments. Theories abound as to why the shepherd is more prone to these particular conditions than other breeds; however, no conclusive veterinary research to date has pinpointed the causes for these conditions.

 Fact

Heavy flea infestations are completely avoidable if the shepherd is well cared for and receives monthly flea killer/repellent as prescribed by a veterinarian. This is one of the most controllable problems your dog might suffer.

The fact that these mystery illnesses do occur in the German shepherd is reason enough to speak with your veterinarian as to what she feels is the best way to prevent these conditions from occurring. You should also ask about treatments she has found effective in controlling these illnesses when they do occur in the shepherd.

▲ Keep an eye out for flea and tick infestations,
especially if your dog spends a lot of time outdoors.

Eye Disorders

Though the shepherd is often considered a breed without eye problems, this is actually not true. Eye disease is ranked as sixth in the list of the top ten diseases that occur more frequently in the German shepherd than in other breeds.

Fact

The eye disease most commonly seen in shepherds is pannus, which is a chronic inflammation of the cornea and, sometimes, the dog's third eyelid. It primarily strikes German shepherds, usually when the dog is middle-aged. Pannus is not generally painful; however, it often results in blindness.

The Canine Eye Registry Foundation (CERF) reports that German shepherds are at risk for eight different types of hereditary eye disease. The presence of any of four diseases—pannus, cataracts (congenital and cortical), retinal atrophy, and optic nerve hypoplasia—will result in a dog's exclusion from CERF and should disqualify a dog from being bred. The presence of the other four diseases—distichiasis, corneal dystrophy, retinal dysplasia, and micropapilla—are allowable, though CERF will issue the warning to breed only to German shepherds without these diseases.

Musculoskeletal Conditions

At one time, the words "German shepherd" immediately brought the words "hip dysplasia" to mind. Even today, the German shepherd is still plagued with this horrendous hip condition. According to some estimates, the German shepherd is more than twice as likely to suffer form hip dysplasia than any other member of the general dog population.

Part of the situation is blamed on the poor hip-muscle development in German shepherds, which can be substantially less than that seen in other breeds. The primary cause of this disease is joint laxity, or the looseness of the joint fit. If the ball end of the femur can move around in the receiving socket of the pelvis, it is more apt to be damaged and heal roughly than in the tight-fitting joint.

 Essential

Hip dysplasia is considered to involve a hereditary factor, which is why it is important to purchase a puppy that not only comes from OFA-approved German shepherds without any hip dysplasia present, but also from parents, grandparents, and great-grandparents with disease-free hips.

Hip dysplasia causes inflammation, pain, and lameness. If severe enough, the shepherd may require surgery to replace the hip joint. It's all very expensive, as well as heart-wrenching for the owner who has to go through this with her shepherd. With as many as one in five shepherds suffering from the disease (ranging from mild cases to severe), canine hip dysplasia is definitely something to watch out for in your dog, not to mention a reason to keep him in good shape. You'll want to develop his hindquarter muscles and keep him at a healthy weight to prevent stress on his hips.

Elbow Dysplasia

This disease is not one that is commonly tested for in the German shepherd; however, many shepherds do suffer from it. Though soreness in the elbow can have a variety of causes, this condition is generally the result of osteochondrosis dissecans (OCD).

Fact

Another location that can suffer from OCD is the German shepherd's stifle joint, or the knee of the rear leg. Keep an eye out for any unsteadiness or favoring of one leg as indications of this condition.

OCD is a disease affecting the cartilage in a joint. Over time, fissures in the cartilage cause flaps to form, and these are exposed to the bones of the joint. This causes inflammation, pain, lameness in the affected leg, and arthritis.

Additional Joint and Bone Problems

German shepherds have the unfortunate status of being one of four primary breeds that are affected by a disease called hypertrophic osteodystrophy. The most unfortunate part is that not much is known about this disease. What is known is that it comes and goes, and when the disease is active, it causes inflammation and lameness in the wrist areas of the dog's front and/ or rear legs. Additionally, dogs affected with this disease may become anorexic, feverish, and depressed and may lose significant amounts of weight.

Sadly, there's more. The German shepherd is *the* breed that is most affected by panosteitus, another condition that affects the leg bones, causing the marrow cavity to become more dense in affected legs. A dog with panosteitus will suddenly appear lame, but the lameness can shift from leg to leg. There's no treatment for this disease other than providing anti-inflammatory treatments and pain medications to make the shepherd more comfortable. Fortunately, though, panosteitus appears to be self-limiting, in that it does not completely degenerate the leg bones.

Osteoarthritis is perhaps the disease most often seen in elderly shepherds, or those aged ten years and older. Cartilage provides a cushion between bones in joints. When this cartilage wears thin, the result is pain, stiffness, and inflammation. It is a natural process of aging. Keeping your shepherd light and fit will aid in warding off this degenerative disease. Additionally, supplements such as glucosamine and chondroiton sulfate have shown promise in slowing the process and easing joint pain.

Skin

German shepherds frequently have skin problems. Two skin disorders that are commonly seen in shepherds are lick granulomas (acral lick dermatitis) and allergic dermatitis. Lick granulomas are raw open areas resulting from a shepherd's excessive licking in one area, removing several layers of skin. German shepherds are notorious for this condition. In the past, the theory was that lick granulomas were the result of a neurotic dog. This may not be so far from the truth; many dogs that are bored, anxious, or stressed do exhibit this damaging behavior.

 Fact

If your shepherd has a flea allergy, it may take only one bite from one flea to initiate an allergic response. This is the one allergy, however, that can be easily controlled. Certain tick and flea medications not only kill all life stages of the flea, but also repel fleas to the point where one may not even hop onto your shepherd.

German shepherds are also one of the breeds noted for the high appearance of allergies. Inhalant allergies, food allergies, and flea allergies will all show up as itchiness in the dog's skin. Dogs do not sneeze and sniffle as people with inhalant allergies do; rather, they will chew, lick, and scratch themselves, sometimes resulting in secondary bacterial infections.

The most common locations for dogs to itch are their paws, armpits, groin, flanks, ears, and heads. To determine what is causing a shepherd's allergies, a specialist will need to test the dog. Once the underlying allergy is determined, the shepherd can be treated much more effectively.

Serious Skin Issues

Two skin conditions that plague the German shepherd almost exclusively are nodular dermatofibrosis and perianal fistula. Nodular dermatofibrosis appears innocuously as lumps on the shepherd's head, neck, legs, and/or between her toes. Unless the lump ulcerates or breaks open, the condition is not considered painful for the dog. If a shepherd has this condition, however, she must be tested every three months for the presence of malignant kidney tumors—or, in the case of an intact female, uterine cancer. The type of kidney tumor that develops is cystadenocarcinoma, which is highly aggressive and requires immediate surgery to remove the tumors if the shepherd is to have any chance of recovering.

 Question?

Is the chronic infection on the bridge of a shepherd's nose really caused by digging or rooting in the dirt?
Nasal pyoderma was once considered to be a disease of long-nosed breeds, such as the shepherd, and was blamed on digging or rooting behavior. It is now thought to be an immune disorder. Your veterinarian will be able to offer you the latest therapies available.

Perianal fistula or perianal pyoderma is most common to German shepherds and Irish setters. Though this disease appears to be a horrid bacterial infection (causing draining lesions surrounding the shepherd's anus), it isn't bacterial at all. For years, veterinarians tried to treat this disease with antibiotics—with no lasting response. Surgeries have had marginal success.

Researchers continue to delve into this painful condition; hopefully an effective therapy will be developed in the near future.

Heart

Few informational sources list heart disorders as a problem with the German shepherd. However, veterinary research paints a different picture. The German shepherd is recognized as being at significantly greater risk of suffering from patent ductus arteriosus (PDA), subaortic stenosis (SAS), and persistent right aortic arch (PRAA).

PDA is the most common congenital heart condition in dogs. It occurs most frequently in females and is, in simple terms, a hole in the heart that never closed while the puppy was developing in the uterus. The hole shunts blood into the dog's lungs and away from the rest of her body; it must be surgically corrected. SAS is the second most common congenital heart defect. With SAS, the blood flow out of the heart is restricted due to an abnormal ring of tissue. Death is usually very sudden and unexpected. PRAA also involves an abnormal tissue ring that restricts blood flow. The most common symptom of this disease is regurgitating all or part of every meal.

The German shepherd may suffer from other heart diseases; however, the breed is not at an elevated risk for any other specific heart problems. All other heart diseases that the German shepherd may have are common to all breeds.

Internal Problems

Internal diseases that the German shepherd has been reported to experience with more frequency than the general dog population include bladder stones, epilepsy, von Willebrand's disease (vWD), a bleeding disorder, and liver disease.

Both epilepsy and vWD have a genetic basis for the shepherd, which means that dogs with these diseases should not be bred. Bladder stones, or urolithiasis, can have a genetic basis in some instances. German shepherds almost exclusively form silicate stones, or uroliths. Liver disease can develop in German shepherds that are unable to assimilate copper and accumulate this metal in the liver. It is thought that this, too, is an inherited defect.

Fortunately, these diseases are fairly rare and uncommonly seen in canines. However, when these diseases do appear, they appear in the German shepherd at a significantly higher rate than other breeds.

Bloat

The causes of gastric dilation-volvulus syndrome (GDV), commonly known as bloat, are not thoroughly understood. Extensive research and reviews of clinical cases have not produced definitive reasons why this often-fatal condition develops in some dogs and not in others. GDV occurs when the stomach fills with gas (gastric dilation), twists (volvulus), and effectively halts the flow of blood from the stomach into the intestines. This in turn cuts off blood flow to the liver, pancreas, and spleen.

Symptoms of bloat include:

- Drooling
- Rapid, shallow breathing
- Restlessness
- Pale, deep red, or blue gums

If your shepherd shows one or more of these symptoms, treat this as an emergency. Your shepherd's chance of survival depends on how quickly you can get to veterinary care.

Exocrine Pancreatic Insufficiency (EPI)

EPI is the atrophying of the part of the pancreas that produces certain digestive enzymes. Without these enzymes, the shepherd cannot metabolize his food, which means he can't pull the necessary nutrients out of his food during digestion. The

German shepherd is the only breed in which EPI has been recognized as being hereditary.

Symptoms of the disease include loose, foul-smelling stools or diarrhea, and a huge appetite coupled with weight loss. Fortunately, this is one disease that is usually easy to treat. Powdered pancreatic enzyme extracts are added to the shepherd's food. If the shepherd doesn't respond well to this therapy, antibiotics may be necessary, as well as vitamin supplementation and a change in diet—all under the careful supervision of a veterinarian.

Cancers

Most people immediately associate the word cancer with death. In the past, this was true. Today, many cancers are treatable if caught early. Sadly, the two cancers to which the German shepherd is predisposed, suffering a significantly higher rate of recorded cases than the general dog population, are hemangiosarcoma and osteosarcoma. Both of these cancers are extremely aggressive and very difficult to treat.

 Essential

Hemangiosarcoma characteristically strikes shepherds that are middle-aged or older, between nine and eleven years old. The German shepherd is the only breed noted as being predisposed to this cancer.

Hemangiosarcoma

This malignant cancer attacks the cells of the blood vessels. Tumors can form literally any place that blood flows, although they are most often found in the spleen. From there, the tumors quickly spread to the liver and heart. Not only does this cancer spread swiftly, but the tumors are filled with blood. When a tumor bursts, the dog is in immediate danger of internal and/or external bleeding.

Symptoms of hemangiosarcoma are basically those that result from the bursting of a tumor: anemia, collapse, pale or white gums, bloated abdomen (from fluids), lumps under the skin, swelling of bones, or bones that are painful to the touch.

Osteosarcoma

This cancer has long been recognized as a killer; it is also the most common type of bone cancer. Osteosarcoma is found more frequently in breeds that typically weigh in excess of fifty pounds. In addition to the German shepherd fitting this weight category, it seems the shepherd is one of the ten breeds most likely to suffer from this cancer.

The prognosis for a shepherd diagnosed with osteosarcoma is bleak. Sometimes, amputation of the affected limb followed by chemotherapy may increase the dog's life span up to ten or twelve months. If the dog is not treated, his life expectancy is only two to four months.

Early symptoms of this bone cancer include lameness, inflammation, and tenderness. Even though you might think that your shepherd is suffering from a little arthritis or perhaps strained ligaments or tendons in his leg, go to your veterinarian immediately. By the time your shepherd is showing additional symptoms, such as coughing, breathing difficulties, tiring easily, or not tolerating exercise at all, the cancer may have already metastasized, or spread to other areas of the body.

In general, it is difficult to spot initial signs of some cancers in dogs. The best way to keep on top of your dog's condition is to take him for regular check-ups with a veterinarian. This trained professional will be more sensitive to early signs and symptoms than you will.

Competitive Sports for Your Shepherd

THE GERMAN SHEPHERD IS PERHAPS ONE of the most versatile dog breeds. Not only is he capable of participating in and performing well in every sport that is open to all breeds, he also maintains the inherent drives to train and compete in herding trials. The mediocre shepherd, when it comes to performance sports, is usually the exception rather than the rule. Why not pick a sport and try something new with your shepherd?

Agility

This sport is fast paced and fun, which is part of the reason why agility caught on so quickly and converted so many owners and dogs in such a short period of time. Many dog owners begin training in agility just for fun. This mentality often lasts only until the first competition, when you realize that agility trials are fun, too.

Part of what makes this sport so entertaining is that shepherds *love* the challenge of flying through an obstacle course under the direction and coaching of their handlers. Obstacles may include tunnels, suspended tires to jump through, teeter-totters, A-frames, and a line of poles through which the dog weaves. The American Kennel Club (AKC), North American Dog Agility Council (NADAC), and the United States Dog Agility Association (USDAA) all hold agility events, and all are very similar in judging and structure. Basically, the classes are judged on the dog's completion of the course, with deductions made for knocking down poles, avoiding an obstacle, or not hitting a precise marker when coming off a ramp. If there is a tie between competitors, the dogs' times are used to determine placements. As you might have guessed, faster is better.

What keeps the event fresh for handlers is that every course at every agility trial is different. The potential combinations of obstacles and course layouts are virtually infinite, so the sport never gets stale. Intelligent breeds like the shepherd don't know the exercises by heart, as they often do in obedience.

▲ Jumping is an important part of your dog's agility.

Agility does require a shepherd that is healthy and not suffering from any musculoskeletal diseases. It is also easiest to start out in the sport if you can locate a nearby agility club or training class. In this way, you can receive experienced instruction and have access to the complete array of obstacles without having to build or obtain them yourself.

Conformation

Conformation is the sport of the beautiful—no talent is required, per se, other than that with which the shepherd was born. Looks are everything in this sport. If a shepherd doesn't have exceptional conformation and movement, he may still be a great companion and a tremendous competitor in sports; however, he won't even be considered in the show ring. In fact, if he has a disqualifying fault, such as a white coat, he will not be allowed to enter.

You may think this sounds harsh, but this is the place for judging how closely a shepherd meets the breed standard for conformation and gait, or movement. Dogs that are registered with the AKC may enter any number of classes, such as puppy (dogs between six and twelve months), bred by exhibitor (limited to dogs handled by their breeders in the ring), and open (for any shepherd except those already possessing a championship). Male dogs are judged separately from females. The winners of all the male classes are called back into the ring to determine a Winners Dog. Likewise, from all the winners of the female classes, a Winners Bitch is determined.

Question?

If you think your shepherd is exceptionally beautiful, can you show him yourself?

Yes. However, because competition is so fierce among this breed, you will need to be as polished in the ring as a professional handler. Even then, you can expect that it will take longer to earn the number of points you would if you had sent your shepherd away to be handled by a professional who is easily recognizable by the judges.

The Winners Dog and Winners Bitch then return to the ring and are joined by all the specials, or shepherds that already have their championships. From this group, a Best of Breed (BOB) is awarded, and a Best of Opposite Sex (BOS). The BOB continues on and is judged against the BOBs from all other breed members of the Herding Group. The winner of the herding group goes on to compete for Best in Show.

How many points a shepherd is awarded depends on how many dogs he beats. He will also take on the points of any dog he defeats from another breed. So, if he earned two points for becoming Winners Dog, and he then beats the Winners Bitch (that earned three points because of a larger entry) for BOB, this dog will acquire her three points. If he goes on to win Herding Group and one of the dogs he beats is an old English sheepdog BOB that happened to have earned a five-point major, the German shepherd now has earned a five-point major.

Fifteen total points are required to attain a championship from the AKC. Included in these points, the shepherd must have won at least two majors—shows with a breed entry large enough to earn the shepherd three, four, or five championship points—under two different judges.

Flyball

If your shepherd is crazy about balls, this could be a great team sport in which to get involved. Flyball teams are comprised of four dogs and their handlers. One at a time, each dog on the team races down the fifty-one-foot course, jumping over four hurdles along the way. At the end of the course is a box. The dog must stomp on a lever, which causes a tennis ball to be ejected up into the air. The dog must catch the ball and then race back over the hurdles to the starting line. As soon as he crosses the line, the next dog runs the course.

Speed is everything. The team with the fastest overall time wins, after all time penalties have been factored in for dropped balls or missed hurdles. Flyball has roughly 7,000 dogs registered in the United States, and the numbers are rapidly increasing. If there isn't a flyball club in your area, you can call the North

American Flyball Association for information on how to start your own team.

🐕 Fact

Flyball teams often include at least one small dog, such as a Jack Russell terrier. The reason for this is that the heights of the hurdles are set four inches shorter than the shoulder height of the shortest dog on the team—with a minimum height of eight inches. The lower the hurdles, the faster the larger dogs can leap over them.

Freestyle Obedience

For those who enjoy music and are interested in how obedience and your favorite songs can be combined for a canine performance event, canine freestyle or musical canine freestyle might be the sport for you. Both sports require that you develop a routine for you and your dog and set it to music.

Canine freestyle competitions are sponsored by the Canine Freestyle Federation, Inc. (CFF). Events held by the CFF emphasize heeling-based maneuvers that are set to the musical piece of your choice. At the novice level, you are required to perform certain movements within a specified time period; however, you are allowed to perform with your shepherd on leash. The required elements at this level might include such maneuvers as heeling on the right, right and left turns, a circle, and a pivot. The advanced level is performed off leash and requires more maneuvers with greater precision—also set to music.

Musical canine freestyle encourages costumes (for both handler and dog) and more elaborate choreography. Events are held by the Musical Dog Sport Association (MDSA) and World Canine Freestyle Organization (WCFO). Dog-and-handler teams are judged on their choice of music, timing, costuming, routine development, and showmanship. The moves can be anything you can dream up—from basic obedience (variations of heeling) to flips, dips, spins, and aerials.

 **Essential**

If you go to see a freestyle obedience demonstration, don't be over-whelmed! The highest levels of competition are truly awe-inspiring; however, everyone started somewhere. With this sport, novices all begin on leash and with very simple, basic routines.

Herding

The modern German shepherd is descended from the finest herding dogs that could be found in Germany in the late 1800s and early 1900s. Even though this breed has served primarily as a working dog for nearly a century, the German shepherd still retains strong herding instincts. This becomes obvious when a young shepherd herds all your children into one room or nips at your ankle to move you to another part of the yard.

Not every shepherd has strong enough instincts or the temperament to become a titled herding dog. If he does have what it takes, the next challenge is yours. Not every owner has the time, the facilities, or the access to trained livestock (those that are used to being herded by dogs) to school a shepherd. Ideally, you and your shepherd would be able to train two to three times a week under the tutelage of a herding-dog expert who has experience working with shepherds.

Shepherds can compete in herding trials held by several different organizations: AKC, American Herding Breed Association, and the Australian Shepherd Club of America. All of these organizations hold novice, intermediate, and advanced herding levels. Be warned that even the novice level in this sport requires a substantial amount of practice and experience. Herding is a terrific sport to get involved in with your shepherd, even if you never plan on competing.

Obedience

Obedience is a classic sport. Unlike herding and tracking, which take a dog's natural instincts and talents and mold them into a partnership with the handler, obedience requires that a dog perform exercises for the handler that are completely trained. For example, there is nothing instinctive about heeling. Still, the shepherd is so biddable and so eager to learn, it would be a shame not to put at least a CD title on your dog.

The AKC and the United Kennel Club (UKC) offer obedience titles. The requirements for both organizations are very similar, and most shepherds, with a little additional training, can transition back and forth smoothly between trials. Obedience offers three basic levels: novice, intermediate, and advanced. The titles are: Companion Dog (CD or U-CD), Companion Dog Excellent (CDX or U-CDX), and Utility Dog (UD or U-UD).

 Fact

Performance event judges don't care about color. If you own a white shepherd, you can compete in these events without a problem. In fact, many white shepherds have amassed numerous performance titles over the years.

If you don't enjoy competition, you can still enjoy all levels of obedience. It's almost a guarantee that your shepherd will excel at this sport and will enjoy training with you. So why stop with a basic obedience class? Continue participating until you've reached the utility dog level. At this point, you may have changed your mind about entering trials. If not, you will definitely have the best-trained dog on the block, not to mention an incredible bond with your shepherd.

Rally Obedience

One reason that agility attracted such an enormous following so quickly is that many of the obedience folks were looking for a sport with more variety. When competing in obedience, the exercises, the ring size, and the format are always the same. Finally, some enterprising individual had a brainstorm. First, break down the skills used in individual exercises and mix them all up. Then put these exercises at stations where the required exercise is on a sign. Much like a road rally, the participants can't move to the next station until they've completed the task at the current location.

 **Fact**

The Association of Pet Dog Trainers (APDT) allows both disabled handlers and disabled dogs to compete in rally obedience. If you own a shepherd with hip dysplasia, advanced arthritis, or another condition that compromises his abilities, the APDT will allow you to meet with the judge prior to the class and work out course modifications for your shepherd.

Both the Association of Pet Dog Trainers (APDT) and the AKC offer titles for beginner, intermediate, and advanced levels. (The AKC began its rally obedience program with titles in 2005.) To earn a title, your shepherd will need three passing scores of 170 out of 200 points. Under the rules of both clubs, the highest score with the fastest time wins the class.

Schutzhund

This is a sport that was designed expressly to test the German shepherd's obedience, tracking, and protection abilities, as well as provide handlers and judges with an exceptionally close look at the shepherd's temperament when under extreme stress. This is certainly not the sport for every shepherd, but the shepherd is without a doubt the leader of this sport.

Schutzhund, or VPG, has three levels: SchH/VPG I, SchH/VPG II, and Sch/VPG III. Within each level, there are three separate tests, for obedience, tracking, and protection, which are held over the course of two days. The shepherd must pass each test before he is allowed to participate in the next test. The protection segment of Schutzhund is the final test.

 **Fact**

Schutzhund has something for every shepherd. If you don't want to partake in the protection facet of the sport, you can compete in obedience and/or tracking only. Titles are awarded in both these competitions, as well as awards for the top placements.

Shepherds can test with the United Schutzhund Clubs of America (USA), DVG America, American Working Dog Federation, and the GSDCA-Working Dog Association (WDA).

Working Dog Sport Program

For many years, the AKC would not consider sanctioning any Schutzhund, VPG, or IPO events for German shepherds or any other breed that normally competes in these events. The AKC was very reluctant to allow any bite work, which was largely viewed by the public as training attack dogs. However, nothing could be farther from the truth. A dog with a Schutzhund title—particularly one of the more advanced titles—is a dog with an extremely stable temperament that is very responsive to his handler. In other words, this dog epitomizes courage, intelligence, and control.

 **Essential**

In the past, training methods used by Schutzhund participants have been harsh, potentially creating dogs that were biting out of fear. With today's methods, the dogs see the protective arm of the helper, or the person to be "attacked," as a toy. If he can grab the arm and hold it, the dog is rewarded. It's a game. It's not uncommon to see a shepherd licking the person whom he was holding onto with his teeth just seconds ago.

The GSDCA founded the Working Dog Club to encourage breeders to strive to produce a more versatile shepherd—the dog that is not only built and moves well, but also possesses the temperament and courage that have made the shepherd's century of accomplishments legendary. The GSDCA-WDA was successful; the AKC added the Working Dog Sport Program (WDS) to its proposed titling events in 2004.

As of the printing of this book, the regulations and titling requirements had not yet been published; however, the sport is modeled after the original Schutzhund events. However, the AKC's WDS is going to have a more gradual entry into the sport. WDS will have novice, intermediate, and advanced levels of participation. The highest level—above the advanced level—will be the Master's competition. At the Master's levels (I, II, III) the tests will be equivalent to the three-part Schutzhund tests—I, II, and III.

Other Activities for Your Shepherd

SO YOU DON'T LIKE COMPETING in sports, but you'd still like to do something fun, unique, or exciting with your shepherd? You picked the right breed—the shepherd is capable of participating in a wide range of activities. From helping to brighten a child's day to saving a person's life, there are boundless activities that you and your shepherd can do together to make a real difference. The activity you choose is just a question of where your shepherd's talents lie and how they match up with your personal interests.

Animal-assisted Therapy

The German shepherd has a long and noteworthy record of service to people in need. From serving as highly trained guides for German soldiers blinded by mustard gas in World War I to working as specialized motility, psychiatric, and seizure alert service dogs in present day, the German shepherd has proven his value in many complex and difficult service positions.

Working as a therapy dog requires an unflappable temperament. The shepherd must enjoy being around all kinds of people, be comfortable walking on slick floors, and not startle or become concerned with loud noises. A shepherd that responds fearfully or aggressively when surprised would not be suitable for this work.

Therapy dogs are no longer limited to visiting long-term care facilities to cheer up patients. Rather, these dogs have been recognized for their important role in rehabilitating patients following surgery, serious injury, and failed health. An animal-assisted therapy (AAT) dog is now a vital part of a patient's treatment care plan.

To get involved in this type of work, your shepherd will need to receive his certificate from the AKC stating that he has passed the Canine Good Citizen (CGC) test, described in the next section. Once he has his CGC, you will need to enroll in an AAT training class. These classes are provided by the AAT certifying organization in your community. If you call a few obedience-training clubs, you should be able to locate an AAT class in your area.

Once you and your shepherd have completed this course, you may apply to take the AAT certifying test. This test has two segments: an interview and a performance test. The interview is conducted with a member of the AAT certifying organization. Your shepherd will be with you while you are questioned. The performance test will check your shepherd's reactions to such things as a doctor briskly walking by with a flapping white medical coat, a person inching along in a walker, an approaching individual with an odd, unbalanced gait, a person wearing a surgical cap, mask, and gloves, a person who suddenly shouts loudly and incoherently, and a bed pan being dropped on the floor.

Once certified, you and your shepherd will begin volunteering with an experienced handler and dog. Where you work and what type of work you will be doing depends on the needs in your area and your dog's special talents. AAT dogs work in a myriad of settings, including reading intervention programs, rehabilitation centers, children's hospitals, dementia units, prisons, and long-term care facilities—to name just a few. AAT is extremely rewarding work for both you and your shepherd.

Canine Good Citizen

The AKC initiated a test for all dogs—mixed or pure, registered or not—that acts as a statement of the dog's good temperament and stableness around people. The Canine Good Citizen (CGC) status is not only a requirement before a dog can become certified as an AAT dog, it is also a good certification for all shepherds to possess. When an ignorant neighbor accuses your shepherd of being a dangerous dog for no reason at all, the CGC certificate is a good document to use in your dog's defense. The CGC is an indication of a dog's good temperament and manners. On top of that, it is also proof that you are a responsible dog owner.

Essential

Insurance agencies have been known to deny shepherd owners homeowner's insurance because they own German shepherds, in cases where German shepherds are on the companies' list of dogs causing bite injuries. However, if your shepherd has a CGC, some insurance companies may be more inclined to waive this restriction and insure your home. The CGC certainly doesn't hurt, and it can most likely help.

Shepherds need to be at least four months old to take the CGC. The skills that are necessary to pass include being comfortable around people and strange dogs, as well as walking on a loose leash, walking through a crowd of people, sitting politely for petting, and coming when called. The test is pass/fail and can be taken as many times as needed to achieve a pass. Once a dog passes, his name and registration information (if available) are permanently recorded in the AKC's CGC archives. You will also be given an opportunity to purchase a CGC collar tag to show off your dog's achievement.

To find out more about the CGC and to locate a training preparatory class, contact your local humane society, shelter, or pound. Training clubs in your area should also have information on CGC training classes.

Hiking

The German shepherd is built to work all day. Barring any physical disabilities, virtually every shepherd will enjoy spending a day hiking with his owner. Even shepherds with fears or protective issues that might make them difficult to work with in crowded areas are calmed by the relative isolation of hiking in the wilderness. This is a great opportunity to bond with your shepherd at a relaxed pace in beautiful surroundings.

Alert!

If you enjoy hiking and camping with your shepherd, explain this to your veterinarian. In addition to making sure your shepherd has flea and tick preventive, she may recommend that your shepherd receive additional vaccinations for giardia and Lyme disease, or other diseases that your shepherd could be exposed to in the wilderness. It's always better to be safe than sorry.

However, hiking with your shepherd is not without rules. Most national parks allow dogs; however, they *must* be on leash. This means you will need to work with your shepherd and practice hiking with the dog's leash attached to your pack or waist. You can't hold the leash because you will need your hands and arms for your own balance. Though it sounds easy to have your shepherd's leash attached to you, your shepherd must be responsive to your voice commands so that you can slow him down (so he doesn't drag you up the mountain), recall him (to prevent him from coming in direct contact with dangerous wildlife), and hurry him up (so he doesn't sniff and mark every tree along the way). You also won't want to have him in his regular collar; a well-fitted harness that is smooth and doesn't rub is much more comfortable for the shepherd than wearing a collar attached to a leash that's attached to you.

Your shepherd may need to practice wearing a specialized pack. If you are going to stay overnight along your hiking trail, it is very helpful if your shepherd can carry his own food or water—or both. Your dog will need eight ounces of water for every hour that you will be hiking. Water weight can add up, and carrying this additional weight takes conditioning and practice. The pack will likely be wider than the shepherd, so he will need to practice with it before your actual hike.

Don't forget to plan ahead. If you don't walk your shepherd more than half a mile every other day, you can't expect him to jump off the couch and go for a rugged, three-mile hike on the weekend. Build him up gradually to this distance, making sure to watch for any strained muscles or other signs of lameness.

Public Education

Dog safety is a huge issue in today's society, and yet it is one of many programs that isn't supported financially by many public schools. Many of these schools depend on the benevolence of volunteers from local shelters to offer free dog-safety programs to children. However, shelter staff members are often already spread so thin that they can't possibly cover all the elementary, intermediate, and middle schools in their areas without a lot of help.

This is where you and your shepherd might be of assistance. If your dog loves children of all sizes, doesn't mind being crowded around for pats, and has a wonderful, even temperament, he might be just perfect for a public education job. You will most likely be required to have a CGC certificate and possibly an AAT certification. If the local Humane Society does not have a program in place, consider helping them to develop one that can be offered to the schools. Alternately, you can contact local obedience training clubs and AAT organizations; you might be able to obtain some leads for contacts through these people.

As a public educator, your work would involve teaching children the correct way to treat their own pets: humanely and with kindness. Children also need to recognize some very basic aspects of dog body language. So many children—and even adults—don't recognize the difference between a friendly dog with a gently wagging tail and a taught-bodied dog that is braced to attack. They don't realize that a dog might interpret a kiss on the nose as an act of aggression, or that plopping down on top of a dog is not the same as plopping down on a pillow. Teaching children just a few basics can reduce the number of dog bites substantially—especially if you have their undivided attention, which you will when you walk in with your dog.

 **Fact**

An estimated 800,000 people are bitten by dogs annually. Of this number, more than half are children. In cases of dog bite fatalities, almost all victims are infants or children, with very few teens and adults, and only slightly more elderly people in the statistics. The reason for these high numbers is that very few children are taught how to behave around their own pets, and almost none know how to act around a stray or unfamiliar dog.

If you can teach your shepherd a few tricks to amuse the children, this can be a great icebreaker. It will also help children feel more comfortable around your shepherd. Unfortunately, shepherds are watched with a wary eye, especially among children in urban areas who may not have had good experiences with German shepherds in the past. But your presence as a responsible owner with a well-trained shepherd can break down those stereotypes and help the children learn some valuable lessons.

Search and Rescue

Without question, after the terrorist attacks of September 11, the general public saw just how effective the German shepherd is as an urban search-and-rescue (SAR) dog. Toiling at a grim job for long hours, the German shepherd served not only as an SAR dog but also as an on-the-spot therapy dog during this tragedy. Perhaps this one horrible event has done more to move the public eye toward this heroic breed than anything in the previous half-century.

The German shepherd's visibility during the SAR missions following the attacks brought to the forefront this country's need for more trained dogs and more highly qualified handlers. SAR is not a part-time, weekend pastime. It requires a passion to serve among some of the most dedicated volunteers of all time.

If you are interested in training your dog to search for live searches (lost living people) or cadaver searches in wilderness, urban, and/or water settings, you need to find a volunteer SAR organization in your area. A good way to find the best organization near you is to contact your local sheriff's office or the National Forest Service and ask which SAR unit they call if they need assistance. Then, call the SAR's contact person for information on this unit, and express your interest in training your shepherd for SAR work.

To participate in SAR, your shepherd should be healthy, free of musculoskeletal problems, and an excellent tracking dog. Shepherds that are crazy about balls or tug toys often do well in this line of work; the dog learns that when he finds the source of the scent, a ball is going to magically appear and he gets to play. Tracking may be rugged, hard work for the handler, but if you train your dog correctly, your shepherd will passionately work at this job every single day.

As a handler, you will need to be in excellent physical shape, as well as extremely knowledgeable about wilderness survival, orienteering, and first aid for both you and your dog. You will need to have a flexible job that allows you to respond to SAR calls at any time of day or night and be away for days at a time. You also need to have good nerves, as searches for missing persons often end in the discovery of a corpse. This job is not for the faint of heart, but you will be doing an invaluable service—providing closure to distraught family members, uncovering important evidence, and giving your shepherd the job he needs to thrive.

 **Essential**

Before your shepherd can begin working as an SAR dog, he must be certified as a qualified SAR dog. Every SAR organization has its own certification standards. Generally, there are certifications for live or cadaver/human remains searches. The dog is certified for these searches in specific locations, such as wilderness, urban, or water rescue. Additionally, SAR organizations typically have several levels of expertise within each category.

SAR work is difficult, both physically and emotionally. It can also become expensive; you will rarely be reimbursed for the gas you use driving to search locations. However, SAR work is extremely rewarding. If you have the dog, the time to train, and the desire to perform an important public service, you should look into SAR. You and your shepherd could make a profound difference in someone's life.

Tracking

One of the skills for which the shepherd was bred is tracking. As a police or military K-9, the German shepherd is expected to be able to track the route taken by a person. (The Schutzhund test, specifically designed to challenge the inherent abilities of the German shepherd, includes a difficult tracking segment.) The German shepherd is not a dog that tracks every single step, a skill called trailing. Rather, he uses a combination of skills, including scenting the ground to determine the disturbance created by the footsteps and air-scenting to pick up the direction in which a person moved.

▲ Tracking is a very useful German shepherd skill.

The AKC offers three levels of tracking: Tracking Dog (TD), Tracking Dog Excellent (TDX), and Variable Surface Tracker (VST). A German shepherd that attains all three titles is awarded the AKC's Champion Tracker (CT) title.

At the entry level for tracking (TD), the shepherd must be able to follow a 440-yard track that was laid by a person up to two hours prior to the test. The judge knows where the track goes, but you and your shepherd don't. The track may have as few as three changes in direction or as many as five. You can talk to and encourage your shepherd while you are tracking, but you cannot direct him to go in a specific direction.

You must also remain at least ten feet behind your dog as he navigates through the track. The tracking line has a tie to mark where the required ten-foot distance is for the handler. This long line is attached to the shepherd's harness.

The test is over when the dog either runs out of time or the dog successfully navigates the track and finds the scented item or article at the end of the trail. When the dog finds the object, he is to indicate to the handler that he's found something, usually by going into a down. The dog must not pick up the item until the exercise is over.

Essential

In a police search for a perpetrator, when the K-9 is tracking he must indicate any found items but—as with the tracking test—he must not pick up or disturb this physical evidence in any way.

At the TDX level, the trail left for the dog to track becomes more complicated. Twice as long as the TD test, it now measures half a mile or more. The scent is older, too. The track can be laid three to five hours before the test is run. The TDX test has five to seven changes of directions. A new wrinkle in the test is that a second trail is laid that *crosses* the trail the dog is following. Along the way, the shepherd must indicate three articles, which he must not pick up or disturb.

As difficult as these layouts appear, they are even more difficult in real life. The tracking tests are held in all kinds of weather over all kinds of terrain. The handler must be in as good physical shape as the shepherd. Additionally, the manner in which scent pools in some locations, drifts in others, and disappears in certain conditions are all complicating factors that challenge even the best tracking dogs.

The final tracking level available through the AKC is the VST test. This test was incorporated into the tracking program to mimic an urban setting in which a person has gone missing or is being sought. The VST is held on all hard, nonvegetative surfaces, such as city sidewalks, streets, metal staircases, and slick indoor floors. The dog must also indicate articles along the way without disturbing them.

If you've never trained a dog to track before, finding a local tracking club will be very beneficial. Don't shy away from this sport if your shepherd is no longer a puppy. Though tracking folks recommend beginning with young puppies in this sport, the older shepherd will pick it up quickly and enjoy every minute.

Active Shepherds Make Enjoyable Companions

Obviously, this chapter is not a definitive summary of all the activities you can enjoy with your shepherd. It's just the beginning. Depending on your shepherd's abilities, you might enjoy looking into disk catching, weight pulling, or carting. The German shepherd is capable and willing to do all of these activities. You might also enjoy taking him with you when you go fishing or for an afternoon boating on a lake.

One thing is for sure. The more active you keep your shepherd, the more enjoyable it will be to live with him and spend time with him. The more you appreciate your shepherd, the deeper your bond will become. Isn't that what owning a dog is all about?

Traveling with Your Shepherd

YOUR GERMAN SHEPHERD LOVES TO BE where you are. If you're driving to the park, she'll do anything to get in the car and tag along. If you're planning a weekend in the mountains, she'll think that's a great idea, too. Whether traveling by car, train, boat, or plane, if she's allowed to ride with you and your travel plans will accommodate her, you'll make your shepherd very happy if you take her along.

The Importance of Identification

If you are planning to travel with your shepherd, it is critical that she is identifiable. If your shepherd accidentally gets loose, lost, or is stolen, there's very little chance that you'll see her again if she doesn't have some form of identification on her. Obviously, she can't carry around an identification card; however, there are several options available that can contain just about as much information. Some are temporary forms of ID, such as tags and collar plates. Other forms of ID are permanent, such as tattoos and microchips. All these forms have their pros and cons, and what works for you may be different than what might work for another owner.

Identification Tags

Your dog can be identified by her rabies tag or by her city license tag, if she has one. Your shepherd can also be identified by her personal tag, which should list a telephone number at which you can easily be reached—most likely a cell phone number.

Question?

Why would you want to list your cell phone number on your dog's personal tag?
If you are traveling and your dog is lost, you won't be at home to receive any calls about her whereabouts until you are back home. With your cell phone number listed, you can take calls regarding your shepherd while you are still in the area and have the best chance of finding her.

The danger in ID tags is that they do fall off. If the tag catches on something, the little ring that connects it to the collar is going to break before the collar does. A brass collar plate engraved with your dog's name and your cell phone number stands a better chance staying intact with the collar; however, neither a tag nor a collar plate will be helpful if your shepherd's collar comes off.

Tattoos

A permanent form of identification is a tattoo. The shepherd's AKC registration or ILP number is tattooed on the dog's inner thigh. Tattoo numbers can be registered with the AKC, as well as one of several national registries that maintain tattoo numbers and contact information for a small fee.

The biggest drawback to the tattoo is that the average person won't know how to use this information to return your dog to you. In fact, the average person may not even see the tattoo. In preparation for applying the tattoo, the shepherd's inner thigh is shaved.

When the hair grows back, the tattoo may not be readily visible. Additionally, if a young puppy is tattooed, as he grows the tattoo could become stretched and distorted—making it nearly impossible to read the numbers.

Microchips

A microchip is a permanent form of identification that is about the size of a small grain of rice. It is imbedded between the dog's shoulder blades. The microchip contains a number that can be read using a special chip scanner. When the microchip company receives a call from the shelter or veterinarian scanning the dog, they will be able to put the rescuer in contact with you and vice versa.

Drawbacks to the microchip are that it's not obvious that a dog is microchipped, and a good Samaritan wouldn't know the dog is identified just by looking at him. Only shelters and veterinarians with scanners can identify the chip, but not every shelter and veterinarian has a scanner. Furthermore, the chip may migrate farther down the shoulder, so if the dog is scanned in the wrong spot, it may appear as if he doesn't have a chip.

If a chip may not be scanned, a tattoo might be overlooked, and a tag might be lost, what is the solution? Typically, a combination of IDs, such as a tag and a tattoo or a collar plate and a microchip or even *all* forms of ID (tag, tattoo, and microchip), will cover the bases for even the most-traveled shepherd.

Hotel Stays

As more pet owners are traveling with their dogs, an increasing number of hotels, motels, and B & Bs are now accepting reservations for owners and their dogs. Typically, an additional fee is charged for the dog to stay in the room with you. Additionally, a hotel may ask for a deposit for damages. If your shepherd doesn't wreck the room, your credit card won't be charged. If the room is damaged, the hotel can charge you the full deposit fee.

To prevent your shepherd from causing any damage, keep him crated when you have to leave your room. Do not leave him in a mesh crate; he can chew out of this quickly. Additionally, hang the Do Not Disturb sign on the door to your room. You do not want anyone entering the hotel room while your shepherd is unattended. You definitely don't want your dog loose in your room if there's any chance for destruction—or if a hotel staff person might open your door. Entering a room with a loose shepherd could either result in an injury, an escaped dog, or both.

While staying in hotels, try to observe good hotel etiquette. Don't allow your shepherd to bark, howl, or whine endlessly in the room while you are gone. Clean up after your shepherd *everywhere*. Don't walk your dog in high-traffic areas; many people do not like dogs or are intimidated by them. If there is a dog-walking area, use this area judiciously. Also keep in mind that every dog (with any number of diseases) that has stayed at that hotel has visited the special dog area. Do you want your shepherd sniffing around in this area? Probably not. If you can find an out-of-the-way place to walk your dog where you can clean up well after him, this may be a wiser choice for your dog's health.

Car Travel

Before you can consider traveling with your shepherd on vacation, he needs to first be able to travel contentedly in the car with you when you run daily errands. This means he must be comfortable with car travel and fully acclimated to whatever restraining system you have chosen for him.

Restraints

A crate in the back of an SUV, station wagon, or minivan is very convenient. Your dog is safe if you stop short; he can't be thrown across the seats or through the windshield. Additionally, you and any passengers are safe; in an accident, a loose dog could seriously injure someone just by being thrown around in the car.

If you don't have a vehicle in which you can fit a crate, consider using a seatbelt harness. Several companies manufacture harnesses that are made to hook through the seatbelt. This allows the dog to sit up, turn around, and lie down comfortably, but he cannot hop from seat to seat. In an accident, your shepherd would not suffer such serious injuries as he would if he were unrestrained.

Fact

Shepherds that initially have a tendency to vomit in the car often can benefit from riding shotgun in the front passenger seat. The seatbelt harness is ideal for a dog in the front seat. Keep in mind, however, that your airbag was not designed for shepherd safety and might impact him in a totally different way.

Climate Control

If you've ever ridden in the back seat of a vehicle, you're acutely aware of how possible it is for the passengers in the front seat to be nice and cool from the air conditioning while you're uncomfortable and even sweating in the back. Keep this in mind when your shepherd is riding in the far back end of your vehicle. If his crate is in the cargo area of a minivan, for example, he's getting even less air than the back row of seats. Always make sure he's not becoming overheated during travel. If necessary, attach a battery-powered fan to his crate to help the air flow.

Never leave your shepherd in the car on a hot or even warm day. It takes only a matter of minutes for the car to heat up to an unbearable temperature. If you are traveling on a hot day and making a rest stop, take your shepherd out to walk in the shade, stretch his legs, and relieve himself. If you are making a lunch stop and plan to go inside the restaurant, allow the car engine to keep running with the air conditioning on. Or, better yet, get your meal to go.

The Anxious Traveler

Owners often decide to take the family dog with them on a fun trip, maybe to see a relative who lives six hours away, failing to consider that the dog has never ridden in the car except to go to veterinary appointments, where he got vaccinations that hurt. The dog is simply not going to hop in and enjoy the ride. The less-traveled dog is likely to pant, cry, whine, bark, vomit, and possibly even lose bowel or bladder control. Putting a shepherd in this situation isn't fair. Your dog's nervous behavior is also guaranteed to wear thin on all who are traveling with you.

▲ After a long travel period, make sure your pet gets a lot of exercise.

To prepare your shepherd for a journey, you need to make sure he considers his crate a safe haven. Keep his crate in the home, door open, and encourage him to go in the crate to receive treats and enjoy really good chew toys and bones. When he's comfortable with the crate, begin taking short trips in the car.

Give your shepherd his favorite chew toy or bone so he has something to do in the crate. Initially, you may want to line the crate with newspapers for easier cleanup. Also, take him on short trips as frequently as possible. Over time he will become more used to the motion of the car and will be less apt to become ill. If you take him to a pleasurable place (such as a park), he will connect the car rides with good things. This will help, too. Eventually, he will undoubtedly be first in line at the door when you ask, "Does anyone want to go for a car ride?"

 Essential

Resist the urge to try to soothe your nervous shepherd with calming words. He will misinterpret this as praise for being nervous, which will exacerbate the situation. Also, no matter how whiny and annoying he gets, don't yell at him. This could also make the situation much worse. The best plan is to ignore him until he is calm, and then you can praise him.

Air Travel

Your shepherd will only be able to travel with you on an airplane if he fits into one of two categories. One is if he is your own certified service dog and must be with you at all times. The other is if he's a puppy and is still small enough to fit in an airline-approved in-cabin carrier.

If you are traveling via airplane to pick up your shepherd puppy from the breeder, you should make arrangements with the airline well in advance of your flight to bring your puppy in the cabin with you. To do this, you'll need your breeder to obtain a health certificate for the puppy from her veterinarian stating that the puppy is healthy and able to fly.

You will need to call your airline and make reservations for your new puppy. You'll be asked to pay for the puppy's passage, which could be anywhere from $50 to $80 or even more, depending on the airline. Your puppy will receive his own ticket that you must present at boarding.

Due to tighter flying restrictions, you can expect the employees at the counter to inspect your puppy's carrier to make sure that it meets their travel standards and fits your puppy. Your shepherd must be able to stand up, turn around, and lie down comfortably.

While in the airplane, you'll be required to keep the puppy in his carrier at all times, and the carrier must remain under the cabin seat in front of you.

Canine Cargo

If you can avoid it, do not have your shepherd fly cargo. Though the airlines that ship dogs in the cargo hold make a sincere effort to ensure that your shepherd is safe from take-off to destination and all points in between, flying a dog in cargo puts your dog at greater risk of being seriously rattled or even killed.

 Essential

If flying your shepherd in cargo is absolutely unavoidable, make sure you do everything possible to make your shepherd's trip safe. Regulations and restrictions for the travel of domestic animals are constantly changing. Some airlines place restrictions on the breeds that they will fly. Call the airline and find out exactly what is required to safely ship your dog in cargo.

For one thing, it's very noisy in the cargo area. This can be very alarming to shepherds that tend to be a little anxious anyway. If the flight is rough, luggage and shipping items can shift and fall. Depending on the weight of the items, it is possible for a very heavy item to break your shepherd's crate; however, this is unlikely because the airlines require that air travel crates meet specific parameters. These crates are designed to survive very heavy objects falling on top of them.

Other potential problems include having your dog placed in the same cargo hold as a food shipment packed in dry ice. In this case, the oxygen could be depleted and your shepherd could be asphyxiated. If the heating system fails in cargo, your shepherd would quickly freeze to death.

Fortunately, air travel usually goes right many more times than it goes wrong. Of course, if it goes wrong just once and it happens to be your shepherd, it becomes a tragedy. The only reason you should put your shepherd in cargo is if you are moving overseas or attending a competitive event that you can't reach by car without giving up your day job. In all other cases, keep your shepherd's best interests in mind and drive to your destinations.

Finding the Right Boarding Kennel

Whether for business or leisure, there will be times when your dog can't accompany you on your travels. Of course, your best option in this situation is to leave the dog with a responsible friend or relative with whom your shepherd is comfortable. If this is not possible, you'll need to look into some alternatives.

The facility that is most often used by pet owners in this case is a boarding kennel. Boarding kennels range from five-star facilities that offer private suites for your dog, couches, televisions, massages, pool time, lessons in agility, and much more. Whatever you want for your shepherd while you are away, this facility will be able to provide it.

The next level of boarding kennels are well-run facilities that don't have quite as many frills and extras as the more elaborate boarding kennels; however, this level still offers services to meet your shepherd's needs and is more moderately priced. Some kennels may offer housing in an indoor/outdoor run giving the dog the ability to go in and out at will. Other kennels may keep the dogs in large, roomy indoor kennel areas; however, each dog must be taken out to relieve himself, exercise, and play. Options that cost extra could include leash walking for thirty minutes, a special play session, or feeding a particular diet. Still other kennels may offer only the basics: a clean, dry place to sleep and an outdoor exercise pen.

 **Alert!**

Boarding facilities do not allow puppies to be boarded unless they have received a complete course of puppy vaccinations, which usually isn't until the puppy has reached fourteen to sixteen weeks of age. The reason for this is that it is easy to unwittingly expose a vulnerable puppy to a lethal virus.

Before you make reservations for your shepherd to be boarded, visit several facilities that have received good referrals from your veterinarian, friends, and other dog owners. Look for immaculate runs and helpful staff. Ask questions about how often the dogs are exercised, what types of services the facility offers, if your shepherd can be fed his regular diet prepared according to your instructions (if you provide the food), what the facility's fees are and how they charge for add-on services, and pick-up and drop-off times.

If you are uneasy about anything concerning the boarding facility, or if the operators can't answer your questions to calm your apprehension, do not board your shepherd at this facility. Go with your gut instincts and find another location.

Working with a Pet Sitter

If you can trust your shepherd to stay alone in your apartment or home without tearing anything up, and if she will be fine with only three opportunities per day to relieve herself, a pet sitter might be a good option for you.

A pet sitter will come to your home and offer pet services personalized to your shepherd's needs. This person will feed, water, and walk your dog. He will also play with your shepherd, brush her, and give her medications (if prescribed). Additionally, he will bring in the newspaper, retrieve your mail, turn lights on and off, and open and close blinds—whatever you specify.

 **Alert!**

For a pet sitter to be a viable option, your shepherd must be trusted to allow him into your home. Your pet sitter must also be comfortable caring for a German shepherd. If your dog intimidates the pet sitter, the dog is apt to take advantage of this.

A pet sitter will usually spend between thirty minutes to an hour with your shepherd during a visit. He will charge a fee per visit, which could range from $10 to $12 or more, depending on the going rates in your area. Before you hire him, the pet sitter will come out to meet you and your shepherd and write up a contract. Make sure that you have a system in place so that the pet sitter will continue caring for your dog even if you don't come home when scheduled.

While hiring a pet sitter is a great option for short trips, you don't want to rely on his services for an extended period of time. A dog of any breed—but especially a German shepherd—will become bored if left alone in the house for more than a few days. Even though the pet sitter will come over a few times a day, the shepherd will still be aware that she is alone. Keep these trips short, and get back to your shepherd as soon as you can.

Planning for the Unknown

Severe weather, changes in travel plans, and vehicle breakdowns can all influence whether you are able to return home according to your original schedule. If you have your shepherd at a boarding facility, he's not going anywhere until you can pick him up. If you have employed a pet sitter to care for your shepherd while you are gone and can't get in contact with her, she should be prepared to continue taking care of your shepherd until you have safely returned home. If the sitter leaves her key on the table thinking that you are arriving that evening, a delay in your return could leave your shepherd lonely and hungry.

Additionally, double-check that the emergency contact information you leave with your shepherd's caretaker is current and accurate. The contact that you list should be someone who knows you well, knows your dog well, and will know exactly what to do if something serious happens to you. No one can anticipate a car accident, a sudden and serious illness or injury, or death. However, for your shepherd's sake, it is important that your emergency contact knows your desires for the dog should you be separated from him for a great length of time or permanently.

Dogs are considered property, and therefore they cannot receive any inheritance. But if you want to ensure that your dog is provided for should the unthinkable happen, make sure that the person you've asked to take your dog really wants him. Often, just to be kind, friends or relatives will say, "Yeah, sure, I'd take him for you." But when the situation becomes real, they are unprepared to follow through with their promise.

If you leave money to someone to care for your dog, they could keep the money and get rid of the dog. If you leave your dog to someone, she doesn't have to accept the dog. Unless you know someone who truly adores your shepherd and would follow through in adopting him, it is wise to make other arrangements. Contact your local German shepherd rescue and ask them questions about willing the dog—with funds to support the rescue—so that they can take him in and place him in an exceptional home.

Though dogs are legally considered property, they're more than this—and they deserve more. Your dog is a member of your family, and he requires just as much love and attention as a person. As long as you keep your shepherd's best interests at heart at all times, you and your dog will always be prepared to handle any situation.

Appendix A

Additional Resources

THE FOLLOWING IS CONTACT INFORMATION for a number of German shepherd organizations. Also included are contact details for various health registries, animal behaviorists, and veterinarians. In case you're interested in any of the innumerable sports and activities that your shepherd could enjoy, there's also a list of each sport's sanctioning organizations with addresses, phone numbers, and Web sites, where available.

Breed Clubs

German Shepherd Dog Club of America
Sharon R. Allbright, Corresponding Secretary
P.O. Box 429
Applegate, CA 95703
📞530-878-2826
sharlen@foothill.net
✍*www.GSDCA.org*

German Shepherd Dog Club of America—Working Dog Association
Joy Schultz, Membership Chairperson
1699 N. Jungle Den Rd. #45
Astor, FL 32102
📞386-749-4574
joy@usa2net.net
✍*www.GSDCA-wda.org*

Verein Für Deutsche Schäferhunde (SV) e.V.
Hauptgeschaeftsstelle
Steinerne Furt 71
86167 Augsburg
Germany 0821-74002-0
✐*www.schaeferhunde.de*

American White Shepherd Association
Jackie Wheeler, Membership Chairperson
jackiwheeler@voyager.net
✐*www.awsaclub.com*

White German Shepherd Dog Club of America
Pat Malinowski, Membership Chairperson
238 Althea Lane
Hopkins, MN 55343
☎952-938-4369
duckpatmal@aol.com
✐*www.wgsdca.org*

White German Shepherd Club International
Carla Coggins, Membership Chairperson
7416 Deer Park Drive
Ft. Worth, TX 76137
☎817-232-5519
membership@whitegermansheph erd.org
✐*www.whitegermanshepherd.org*

All-Breed Registries

American Kennel Club
5880 Centerview Drive, Suite 200
Raleigh, NC 27606-3390
☎919-233-3600
✐*www.akc.org*

American Mixed-Breed Obedience Registry (AMBOR)
179 Niblick Rd, #113
Paso Robles, CA 93446
☎805-226-9275
ambor@amborusa.org
✐*www.amborusa.org*

Canadian Kennel Club
89 Skyway Avenue, Suite 100
Etobicoke, Ontario
M9W 6R4 Canada
☎416-675-5511
✐*www.ckc.ca*

United Kennel Club
100 E. Kilgore Road
Kalamazoo, MI 49001-5598
☎616-343-9020
✐*www.ukcdogs.com*

Health and Behavior

Animal Behaviorists
Animal Behavior Society (ABS)
Indiana University
2611 East 10th Street #170

Bloomington, IN 47408-2603
812-856-5541
aboffice@indiana.edu
www.animalbehavior.org

American College of Veterinary Behaviorists

Dr. Bonnie V. Beaver, Executive Director
Texas A&M University
Department of Small Animal Medicine & Surgery
4474 TAMU
College Station, TX 77843-4474
979-845-2351
bbeaver@cvm.tamu.edu

Disease Registries

Canine Eye Registration Foundation (CERF)

Purdue University
CERF/Lynn Hall
625 Harrison St.
W. Lafayette, IN 47907-2026
765-494-8179
canineeye@purdue.edu
www.vet.purdue.edu

VetCancer Registry (VCR)

Dr. H. Steven Steinberg, Coordinator
The VetCancer Registry
P.O. Box 352, 168 West Main Street
New Market, MD 21774
info@vetcancerregistry.com
www.vetcancerregistry.com

Endocrine Diagnostic Section

Diagnostic Center for Population and Animal Health
4125 Beaumont Road, Room 122
Lansing, MI 48910-8104
517-353-0621

Orthopedic Foundation Association

2300 E. Nifong Blvd.
Columbia, MO 65201-3856
573-442-0418
ofa@offa.org
www.offa.org

Veterinarians

American Animal Hospital Association (AAHA)

P.O. Box 150899
Denver, CO 80215-0899
303-986-2800
info@aahanet.org
www.aahanet.org

American Veterinary Medical Association (AVMA)

1931 North Meacham Road, Suite 100
Schaumburg, IL 60173
847-925-8070
avmainfo@avma.org
www.avma.org

American Holistic Veterinary Medical Association (AHVMA)
Dr. Carvel G. Tiekert, Executive Director
2218 Old Emmorton Road
Bel Air, MD 21015
☎410-569-0795
office@ahvma.org
🖘www.ahvma.org

Activities

Agility
American Kennel Club (see entry for *All-Breed Registries*)

United Kennel Club (see entry for *All-Breed Registries*)

American Mixed-Breed Obedience Registry (see entry for *All-Breed Registries*)

Agility Association of Canada (AAC)
Membership: Arlene Lehmann
16648 Hwy. 48
Stoufille, Ontario L4A 7X4
Canada
☎905-473-3473
alehmann@cherryhillarabs.on.com
🖘www.aac.com

North American Dog Agility Council (NADAC)
1152 South Highway 3

Cataldo, ID 83810
info@nadac.com
🖘www.nadac.com

United States Dog Agility Association (USDAA)
P.O. Box 850955
Richardson, TX 75085-0955
☎972-487-2200
info@usdaa.com
🖘www.usdaa.com

Animal-assisted Therapy
Delta Society
580 Naches Avenue SW, Suite 101
Renton, WA 98055-2297
☎425-917-1114
dianneb@deltasociety.org
🖘www.deltasociety.org/aaat.htm

Therapy Dogs International
88 Bartley Road
Flanders, NJ 07836
☎973-252-9800
tdi@gti.net
🖘www.tdi-dog.org

Canine Good Citizen
American Kennel Club (see entry for *All-Breed Registries*)

Conformation
American Kennel Club (see entry for *All-Breed Registries*)

United Kennel Club (see entry for *All-Breed Registries*)

Flyball
North American Flyball Association (NAFA)
1400 West Devon Avenue #512
Chicago, IL 60660
☎1-800-318-6312
✐*www.flyball.org*

Freestyle Obedience
Canine Freestyle Federation, Inc.
Joan Tennille, President
4207 Minton Dr.
Fairfax, VA 22032
president@canine-freestyle.org
✐*www.canine-freestyle.org*

Musical Dog Sport Association
9211 West Road, Suite 143-238
Houston, TX 77064
MDSA@musicaldogsport.org
✐*www.musicaldogsport.org*

World Canine Freestyle Organization, Inc.
WCFODOGS@aol.com
✐*www.worldcaninefreestyle.org*

Herding
American Herding Breeds Association
Siouxsan Isen, Membership Coordinator

siouxsan@ahba-herding.org
✐*www.ahba-herding.org*
American Kennel Club (see entry for *All-Breed Registries*)

Australian Shepherd Club of America
P.O. Box 3790
Bryan, TX 77805-3790
manager@asca.org
✐*www.asca.org*

Obedience
American Kennel Club (see entry for *All-Breed Registries*)

United Kennel Club (see entry for *All-Breed Registries*)

American Mixed-Breed Obedience Registry (see entry for *All-Breed Registries*)

Rally Obedience
American Kennel Club (see entry for *All-Breed Registries*)

Association of Pet Dog Trainers (APDT)
17000 Commerce Parkway, Suite C
Mt. Laurel, NJ 08054
☎1-800-PET-DOGS (1-800-738-3647)
information@apdt.com
✐*www.apdt.com*

Search and Rescue

The American Rescue Dog Association
P.O. Box 151
Chester, NY 10918
information@ardainc.org
✐www.ardainc.org

The National Search and Rescue Secretariat (NSS)
400-275 Slater Street
Ottawa, Ontario K1A 0K2
Canada
✆1-800-727-9414
✐www.nss.gc.ca

National Association for Search and Rescue (NASAR)
4500 Southgate Place, Suite 100
Chantilly, VA 20151-1714
✆703-222-6277
sardogs@nasar.org
✐www.nasar.org

Schutzhund/VPG/Working Dog Sport

American Kennel Club (see entry for *All-Breed Registries*)

Deutscher Verband der Gebrauchsh undsportvereine (DVG) America
Sandi Purdy, Secretary
2101 S. Westmoreland Rd.
Red Oak, TX 75154
✆972-617-2988

spurdy5718@aol.com
✐www.dvgamerica.com

GSDCA-Working Dog Association
Joy Schultz, Membership
GSDCA-WDA Office
1699 N. Jungle Den Rd. #45
Astor, FL 32102
✆386-749-4574
joy@usa2net.net
✐www.gsdca-wda.org

United Schutzhund Clubs of America
3810 Paule Ave.
St. Louis, MO 63125-1718
✆314-638-9686
✐www.germanshepherddog.org

Tracking

American Kennel Club (*see entry for All-Breed Registries*)

Appendix B

Breed Rescue Information

BREED RESCUES ARE THE NUMBER ONE SOURCE for good adult German shepherds. Keeping track of contact information for German shepherd rescues is the difficult part. Internet Web sites and e-mail addresses frequently change. To make things a bit easier, the American German Shepherd Rescue Association maintains a list of German shepherd rescues complete with current contact information. To find up-to-date information about a German shepherd rescue in your area, use this resource first. If you can't adopt a shepherd, consider making a donation to AGSRA or one of many other individual rescues.

American German Shepherd Rescue Association
Help Line Referral Network: 630-529-7396
www.agsra.com/listings.htm
For additional information, contact Linda Kury
707-994-5241
lindakury@saber.net

For donations, make a check out to AGSRA, Inc. and mail to:
Shirley Briggs O'Brien
6565 Buena Vista Dr.
Magalia, CA 95954

Index

The Everything®
Breed-Specific Serie

THE

EVERYTHING

DACHSHUND

B O O K

A complete guide to raising, training, and caring for your dachshund

Joan Hustace Walker

Trade Paperback, $12.95
ISBN: 1-59337-316-3

With *The Everything® Dachshund Book,* you'll learn all there is to know about this social, friendly canine. From adopting the perfect addition to your family to keeping your dog in top shape, this user-friendly guide is filled with the breed-specific information you need to keep your dachshund happy and healthy for years to come.

The Everything® Yorkshire Terrier Book is the definitive guide to this popular dog. Pet expert Cheryl Smith explores not only the history of this personable breed, but also their mannerisms and necessary day-to-day care.

THE

EVERYTHING

YORKSHIRE TERRIER

B O O K

A complete guide to raising, training, and caring for your Yorkie

Cheryl S. Smith

Winner of the Dog Writers Association Maxwell Medallion for excellence in dog writing

Trade Paperback, $12.95
ISBN: 1-59337-423-2

Available wherever books are sold!

The definitive, must-have guides for the most popular breeds!

The Everything® Golden Retriever Book is a necessity for new and potential golden owners everywhere. Written by Gerilyn and Paul Bielakiewicz, cofounders of Canine University®, this title is packed with professional, breed-specific advice that helps readers raise, care for, and train their golden retrievers safely and successfully.

Trade Paperback, $12.95
ISBN: 1-59337-047-4

Trade Paperback, $12.95
ISBN: 1-59337-048-2

According to the American Kennel Club, the Labrador retriever has been rated as the most popular purebred dog in America for thirteen consecutive years. *The Everything® Labrador Retriever Book* is the perfect introduction to America's most popular pet. This title covers all aspects of dog-rearing, from training, health, history, and much more!

To order, call 800-258-0929, or visit us at *www.everything.com*

Trade Paperback, $12.95
ISBN: 1-59337-121-7

The Everything® Poodle Book is your definitive guide to learning how to care for your dog from puppyhood into adulthood. Complete with tips for training your dog to basic health care information, this book gives you all the essential facts you need to understand your pet's needs.

With *The Everything® Pug Book* you'll learn all there is to know about your best friend! From adoption methods and training techniques, to specific tips on diet, exercise, and basic care, you can anticipate your Pug's every need and be prepared for any situation.

Trade Paperback, $12.95
ISBN: 1-59337-314-7

Trade Paperback, $12.95
ISBN: 1-59337-122-5

The Everything® Rottweiler Book tells you everything you need to know about making a rottweiler part of your life. This handy book is an all-inclusive work, covering all aspects of rottweiler care, so you know what to expect and can watch out for issues before they become serious problems.